V. SACKVILLE-WEST

THE ILLUSTRATED

GARDEN BOOK

V. SACKVILLE-WEST

—THE ILLUSTRATED—
GARDEN BOOK

—A NEW ANTHOLOGY BY—
ROBIN LANE FOX

Illustrations by
FREDA TITFORD

Photographs by
KEN KIRKWOOD

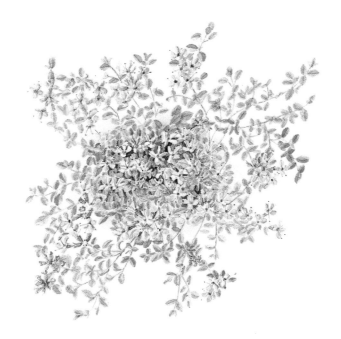

Atheneum · New York · 1989

Produced, edited and designed by
Shuckburgh Reynolds Limited
289 Westbourne Grove,
London W11 2QA

Atheneum
Macmillan Publishing Company
866 Third Avenue, New York, N.Y. 10022

Library of Congress Catalog Card Number: 88-32913

ISBN 0-689-70816-5

Macmillan books are available at special discounts for bulk purchases
for sales promotions, premiums, fund-raising, or educational use.
For details, contact:

Special Sales Director
Macmillan Publishing Company
866 Third Avenue
New York, N.Y. 10022

10 9 8 7 6 5 4 3 2 1

Typeset by SX Composing Ltd, Rayleigh, Essex
Colour separation by Fotographics Ltd.
Printed and bound in Italy by Mondadori

CONTENTS

◆

 *I*NTRODUCTION

For nearly fifteen years, Vita Sackville-West enchanted readers of the *Observer* newspaper with her weekly column on gardening. Writers on gardening need two very different skills: they must be able to garden and also to write. Vita Sackville-West had been a writer since her youth, a poet, novelist and biographer. She and her husband, Harold Nicolson, had already made the great garden at Sissinghurst Castle in Kent: her readers always knew that she was busy with the ideas she suggested and that she wrote with the authority of a great garden-maker and planter. She also contrived a style, a simple, personal tone with literary allusions and an artful air of romance. Thousands of non-gardeners read her articles too, just because they were so good. There had never been such a gardening column and until she stopped, in 1961, her readers gave weekly proof of it. They wrote to her: they sent her seeds, ideas and presents. "I'll give you *Dianthus barbatus magnificus* . . . A border of about 200 in full flower this summer has caused astonishment. It is one of the dear old cottage garden plants that was almost lost. *You* may have it . . .". When she sent plants in reply, they thanked her in the romantic idiom which seemed appropriate: "to be offered a rose by a great poetess as the morning sun lights up the breakfast-table is a delightful experience . . .". In rationed, post-war Britain, they sent her knick-knacks for her own garden, advice on how to keep sparrows off primroses and requests for inspiration with their own designs. When she wrote a beguiling praise of the Chabaud carnation (page 32 of this book), she was over-whelmed with so many letters that it took two weeks to answer them. When she wrote enthusiastically about the unusual strawberry tree the Post Office had to send a special van to Sissinghurst in order to deliver the bags of readers' inquiries.

The tower seen from the White Garden, showing *Rosa* 'Iceberg' (left), *Rosa longicuspes* (right) and *Chrysanthemum foeniculaceum.*

Vita Sackville-West claimed to dislike what she wrote and only continued, she sometimes said, for the money: fifteen guineas a week in the early 1950s was better than the going rate nowadays. She wished to be judged and remembered by her novels and above all, her poetry: "I get furious when people drag up *The Edwardians*, and of course the *Observer* is worst of all ...". She called these pieces the "sticklebacks", yet she did help to perpetuate them by allowing them to be reprinted, prickles and all. During her years in newsprint, four selections of the sticklebacks appeared and were each issued and re-issued to meet the demand. She cannot have wholly disliked her success and the contact with so many readers. She would, I hope, be pleased, though perhaps secretly pleased, that so many people still ask for the articles' whereabouts, regret their passing and as new generations of gardeners grow up, wonder what ideas she had. Their advice and style have not become outdated.

It has given me a particular pleasure to compile and revise a new selection. Twenty-five years ago, I read the first of her own selections as a boy at boarding-school, having borrowed it from the public library. It struck me, as it had already struck so many others, as a bewitching book of ideas and observations. It opened a world of plants and possibilities which I wished to see and try and which I could imagine, meanwhile, in the charmed setting of the distant summer holidays and the years when, finally, I would be free to see gardens and the countryside in June and early July. My own gardening had centred on August, yet here was a book telling me that August could never compare with the youth and greenness of May and early June. It all lay before me: "from March to the end of April is youth, from May to June is middle youth; after the end of July, we enter the painful stage when we know we are going on for sixty ...". I had begun in the year's late middle age.

I have chosen this book from the original *Observer* articles, bringing some of the plant names up to date and changing a phrase or removing a dated reference and sometimes, running two different pieces on one and the same plant into a continuous whole. When choosing, I did not consult her own four books of selections, although inevitably, we overlap at times, nor did I turn to the shorter single volume, edited after her death by her daughter-in-law, Philippa Nicolson. Many of the pieces, therefore, have not been re-issued since their Sunday début. I have tried to convey the various qualities of the entire series by giving each of the main types some space.

To me, as to many others, these articles are a magical lesson in looking closely at flowers, in loving old roses, planting informally within a formal plan, overlooking no plant as too ordinary and tolerating no plant simply because it is already in the garden. Above all, they are an incitement to use the imagination, both in trying to give a garden an air of happy accident and apparently natural romance and also in recalling the moments which all keen gardeners relish. These articles put into words experiences which are otherwise solitary, such as dead-heading roses on late summer evenings, prowling in the half-light in evenings on the edge of spring and summer, sitting and thinking in late autumn about how to make the next improvement. "The major disadvantage of having a garden and working on it is that one leaves oneself with no leisure to study the result one has laboriously achieved or, more likely, failed to achieve . . .". To the end, Sissinghurst was being improved and changed: her husband, Harold Nicolson, aptly entitled his notebook of the plantings in his own special area, the Lime Walk, *My Life's Work*. He knew it would never be finished.

In 1955, Vita Sackville-West received the very great honour of the Veitch Memorial Medal from the Royal Horticultural Society. She had never been trained. She had learned by questioning, reading and experimenting and she would have been the last person to claim great authority in botanical identification or knowledge of whole families. A year later, she was diligently taking a correspondence course in horticulture. However, she had a range of personal experience which botanists or parks gardeners could not always match. Simply as gardening advice, these articles stand up on their own merits. I have tried to choose those whose facts have not become too familiar, sometimes through others' repetition. Again and again, I have been impressed by the small observations, that coronillas are scented by day, not night, that the flowers of the acanthus will last for weeks in water, that there is a honey-scented buddleia for November, that the young seedlings of meadow fritillaries lie "flat to the ground when they first come through, looking as angular as a stick-insect and suggesting that a foot has trodden on them and snapped them". There are also the practical experiments, to find how best to prune winter sweet or to prove that *Magnolia grandiflora* really does flower more freely on a sunny wall. Like her readers, she takes pleasure in finding accepted wisdom proved wrong: the daisy-flowered gerberas turn up, flowering wonderfully, in the damp shade of a greenhouse's staging. An expert article in the R.H.S. journal once gave advice on the hand-pollination of the climbing akebia, an unusual plant which is more often suggested than grown. The advice was not borne out by her own plants which she had grown, typically, from a fruit sent through the post by a correspondent.

Gardeners thrive on practical curiosities and the *Observer* articles pass on their fair share: Epsom Salts will protect pinks from rabbits, although the dose must be repeated after heavy rain; arum lilies will flourish in soil used previously for tomato-plants; when removing the dead leaves from potted cyclamen, we must be careful not to tear a strip off the corm. In 1950, gardeners perhaps knew that branches of ribes, or flowering currant, could be picked as early as January and left indoors in water so that they would open their buds in March. By the 1980s, the trick, I fancy, has been forgotten, although it still works, as I discovered last spring. So does the method of lengthening the short stems of the white-flowered Christmas rose, while I have always been grateful for the simple, obvious advice on testing colour groupings which are still under discussion: pick the flowers in question and take them across to the main plant in the combination to see if they go well together. The article on growing clematis horizontally is a masterpiece, but gardeners are still as slow to realize it as they were when it first appeared.

Other gardening columns have had these qualities, although they tend to convey them in a more impersonal, "expert" way. Vita Sackville-West's had something else: they were read not only by fanatical gardeners but by thousands of wishful-thinking fellow-travellers who liked to entertain a good idea and by the many non-gardeners who liked an elegant performance. Old roses brought the best out of her sense of fantasy, purple bourbon roses with aristocratic French names, pink ones with grey leaves or the cream-pinks in which she saw a distinctive beauty: in French, she discovered, *Rosa alba* 'Great Maiden's Blush' was sometimes called 'Cuisse de Nymphe Émue', and "I would suggest only that Cyrano de Bergerac would have appreciated the implication and that any young couple with an immature garden and an even more immature pram-age daughter might well plant the 'Great Maiden', alias 'la Séduisante' . . .".

Vita Sackville-West liked the origins of plants, their associations in medieval literature and the apt quotation from her own wide reading. As in her poetry, she relished the obsolete or expressive "natural" word: lime-trees were lindens; Sissing-hurst's round area of lawn became a "rondel", the nut-walk a "nut-plat"; there were "garths" and "tussie-mussies"; in June, her plants were in full "foison" and she wanted us to talk of a "floraison" of roses in high summer. She used her fancy and wit, but not humour. Sometimes, the style risked sentimentality and sometimes, one feels, there was more than met the eye in its naive air. A visitor to Sissinghurst, wearing amber-coloured spectacles, gave her a charming opening, but perhaps only she remembered how the central character in her novel, *Seducers in Ecuador* (pub-lished in 1924), had put on coloured spectacles so that the "world is changed for him" and he is protected from the sun's "too-realistic glare". Conversation with a "dark man, a foreigner" in a cottage garden allowed her to present his hydrangea to us by its proper name, *paniculata* 'Grandiflora', and evoke an afternoon of curious romance: I "thought that the foreign man, and the circus which passed us with its caravans and the English country garden were all very much of the same thing . . .". Vita Sackville-West had always liked myth-making and fantasy: Spain and the south, the romantic colours of the lost ideal of cottage gardening, gypsies and foreign climes were stimulants to her imagination. Soon after her first meeting with Virginia Woolf, she had elaborated in letters the fantasy that they would go together to gatherings of Spanish gypsies.

These flights of fancy are matched by her bold imagination in designs and the grouping of plants. She makes her sketches of a plan for an odd corner seem irresistible, even to those who will never plant it. One moment, she is turning a disused flat space into a group of birch trees, underplanted with the sweet woodruff she so wisely valued, "like those enormous eiderdowns that one finds in old-fashioned French hotels": "all colour must be excluded, it must all be green and white; cool, symmetrical and severe". At another time, she is conjuring up a "queer, murky, murderous" grouping, best seen when the sky is "lurid with impending thunderstorms". She could transplant ideas from the grandeur of Sissinghurst's setting to a reader's small front garden, suggesting the carpets of anemone and the hedges of 'Rosa Mundi' which her own taste enjoyed. Her ideas on hedges of daphne 'Somerset' or the flowering *Malus hupehensis* still deserve attention and experiment; her fondness for old, familiar flowers among the rarer plantsman's suggestions give her ideas a lasting relevance.

Sissinghurst itself is a sequence of enclosures, each with its own theme, realized in hundreds of groupings and combinations which a small garden can adapt or take as its starting-point, even without paid gardeners and Tudor brick walls. The Sackville-West articles take no stand on social position or advantage. Their readers recognized their presence, naturally, but their author went to some lengths to avoid them. She never mentions Sissinghurst by name. The ideas and plantings which she describes from Sissinghurst are plantings which could be transplanted anywhere, and often have been since: the white garden, the thyme lawn, the herb garden, the schemes of red and yellow or purples and blues. She describes in some detail a red and yellow garden which she has recently seen: she does not say that it is her own, still growing round the South Cottage. She never overawes the reader by referring to her several gardeners or saying, "At Sissinghurst, I find . . ." or "on my walls, these roses are now thirty feet tall".

This manner was consciously adopted, but it was not false modesty: she was self-taught, aware that professional growers and botanists knew so much more and that nurserymen, earning a living, would have cleverer ways of doing things. Like her readers, she saw herself as an amateur in an endless and surprising pursuit. They might well know more than she did and they could help one another on the way. During the *Observer* years, Sissinghurst was open to paying visitors, the "shillingses" as the owners called them, after their entry fee of a shilling. Vita Sackville-West would often stop and talk at length to "shillingses" who asked her questions and whose efforts and interest she admired. It was, admittedly, a relationship whose terms she controlled, but many of the articles have an affinity with talks to the "shillingses". In 1939, before she wrote for the *Observer*, she had acknowledged these "homely souls who will travel fifty miles by 'bus with a fox-terrier on a lead, who will pore over a label, taking notes in a penny note-book . . . Between them and myself a particular form of courtesy survives, a gardener's courtesy in a world where courtesy is giving way to rougher things".

Sissinghurst, Harold Nicolson aptly wrote, has a "succession of privacies: the forecourt, the first arch, the main court, the tower arch, the lawn, the orchard. All a series of escapes from the world, giving the impression of cumulative escape . . .". As the years passed and the emotional turmoils of her early life receded, Vita Sackville-West withdrew ever further from people into this secluded world. In 1949, her husband wrote how she would like "all the servants and gardeners and farm hands to be thrown into a trance like sleeping beauty, and she and her dog and the little robin by the dining-room to be left as the only three moving things at Sissinghurst . . .". The capacity for solitude is common to all keen gardeners and in Vita Sackville-West it became pronounced. The *Observer* years were years of recurrent illnesses, life at Sissinghurst and almost no social contact with a world outside. "I don't understand how people can live in London for choice. Everything seems so unreal and confusing . . .". Already in 1936, an acquaintance had written down his impressions of the appearance which never left her subsequently: "Her eyebrows were heavy, her eyes very dark, her cheeks had a vivid carmine tinge; and she made no effort to disguise the perceptible moustache which Virginia Woolf mentions . . .". She was dressed in long earrings, a lacy shirt, a heavy corduroy jacket, game-keeper's breeches and top-boots laced up to the knee, "Lady Chatterley and her lover rolled into one . . .".

One *Observer* reader was to have his doubts. He wrote to her, "often, from a priory in Sussex, complaining that she was an armchair, library fireside gardener", a charge to which she replied in an elegant *Observer* postscript (printed on page 57). "May I assure him that for the last forty years of my life I have broken my back, my finger-nails and sometimes my heart in the practical pursuit of my favourite occupation?". Writing for the *Observer* was not a new departure into a field she had yet to conquer. Her first gardening column had appeared in the *Evening Standard* in 1924, entitled *Notes on A Late Spring*. In 1933, on Friday evenings, she had given talks on gardening on BBC radio. She wrote country pieces for the *Spectator* and the *New Statesman* and had published a book, *Some Flowers*, in 1937. Before the *Observer* years, she had already made two gardens in Kent, the first at Long Barn, in her thirties, the other at Sissinghurst whose main plan had been agreed very soon after its purchase in 1930 and whose planting had already matured by 1939 on a site which had been a wilderness.

I would like to expose the foundations on which these articles rest by quoting at random from her garden notebooks, kept in the 1930s and still surviving at Sissinghurst. I have picked on autumn 1937, when even Harold Nicolson's critical eye could see that the garden was beginning to be seriously impressive. His wife's notes dwell on improvements, not on past achievements. Line after line of suggestions occupy several pages, some of which are ticked off later or criticised or marked "done" or "ordered" in red crayon. Sissinghurst is the best advertisement for two maxims of garden design: start with a clear design in mind and keep noting its improvements in a durable book throughout the garden's life. Many people nowadays buy garden books as presents, but few of the recipients use them for very long.

I quote at random, adding a few comments in square brackets. "Remember to plough orchard for red clover . . . [In 1936, she had noted the scope for clover seed, sown in grass at 16 to 24 pounds to the imperial acre: wild-flower gardens are not a rediscovery of the 1970s and '80s]. "Plant Crown Imperials all along the moat wall . . . Layer *Viburnum fragrans* . . . Remove all mauve violas from under [Rose] 'Comtesse de Cayla' and add them to those already under 'Shot Silk' roses . . . [One of the scores of corrections of misplaced colours or small details which run through each year's notes] . . . Get the upright rosemary; see Jason Hill, *The Curious Gardener*, p. 94 . . . [a rare allusion to a book's influence, but one, I think, which did appeal to her in several ways] . . . Plant *Lilium rubellum* among blue poppies: they flower at same time . . . [a charming idea, and timing is the essence of all colour groupings] . . . Remove the 'Betty Uprichard' standards from the cottage garden . . . [how interesting that its lovely red and yellow planting began with tall specimens of this salmon and carmine tea rose] . . . Get *Dictamnus fraxinella* (seen at Sutton Courtenay) . . . [the burning bush plant, in the garden of a great plantswoman, Norah Lindsay] . . . Order from Bunyard [E.A.B., her great adviser on roses at this date] 'Queen of

Denmark', '3 Stars', 'Natalie Nypels', 'Oeillet Panachée' – rather washy thing, only worth having one bush of . . . Move seedling of clematis by yew hedge: plant it in the orchard up a dead tree . . . [two Sackville-West hallmarks, the saving of nature's seedlings and the use of climbers up trees; neither is a detail for an over-tidy garden] . . . Plant English iris 'King of the Blues' round [Rose] 'William Lobb' . . . Get *Ceanothus thyrsiflorus*, gentian-blue in August . . . *Lobelia cardinalis* for South Cottage garden . . . [this red-flowered beauty is still represented there] . . . *Lonicera trago-phylla* to climb dead trees in orchard . . . [a lovely choice of the scentless yellow honeysuckle for a lovely unexploited purpose] . . . Sow pansy seed in spring garden paving . . . Plant New Zealand reed-grass round the lake to attract wild duck: order from the Country Gentlemen's Association who recommend it . . . Plant *Iris laevigata* by lake – it doesn't mind water over its roots . . . Wire-brush the old lean-to in the courtyard . . . musk roses for orchard: order from Bunyard [they are still there] . . . produce yew hedge at end of moat [it was not, eventually, yew] . . . combine *Gentiana sino-ornata* with *Ceratostigma willmottianum* . . . [two contrasting blues] . . . *Clerodendron trichotomum*, recomm. by Norah Lindsay [in 1953, her husband, Harold Nicolson, notes at an R.H.S. show for her benefit, the "finest show of jade berries I have ever seen on this shrub"; it clearly became a favourite] . . . The lead virgin [a statue] . . . : put her in the macrocarpa garden under dining-room? . . . [the area later became the White Garden and the lead virgin now stands under the weeping silver pear] . . . New herb garden: grass paths, clematis on trellis at opening . . . [the herb garden still flourishes, with paved paths, but this pleasant idea for clematis was not carried out].

These notes are only a selection, from one season (autumn) in one year: twenty years later, the gentleman in the Sussex priory was mistaking her for "never having performed any single act of gardening herself". In 1937, Sissinghurst was already being tended by four gardeners, under the talented John Vass, the head gardener. It was particularly important to keep such detailed notes when others were at hand to be directed and given the relevant work. The Nicolsons, however, put their own energies into the garden throughout its life.

Where did the style and the ideas come from, people are now beginning to ask? Not long ago a lady told me that she did not think the Nicolsons were really gardeners as they simply copied the ideas out of books and other people's gardens. She ought to have met the man in the Sussex priory; she, too, was completely wrong. Of course, the general style had its forerunners. Vita Sackville-West wrote approvingly of William Robinson, the protagonist of wild and informal flower-gardening who belonged to the previous generation; before she began to make Sissinghurst, she had visited his garden at Gravetye, although it was then passing its peak. She had also visited the famous garden of Miss Jekyll at Munstead as early as August, 1917. It certainly gave her ideas about choosing roses and border plants, although she already had made notes on these subjects, as we shall see. She knew Miss Jekyll's ideas on colour schemes and colour planning, although they, too, were part of a wider Edwardian tradition, only a few memories of which reach us in the great lady's writings.

Miss Jekyll's own garden was not the origin of Sissinghurst. She liked to lead up to strong colours in a border through a spectrum of carefully-chosen shades, a style never followed at Sissinghurst. In *Colour Schemes For The Flower Garden*, published in 1908, Miss Jekyll had given one chapter to "gardens of special colouring", a future characteristic of Sissinghurst. "Occasionally I hear of a garden for blue plants, or a white garden, but I think such ideas are but rarely worked out with the best aims . . .". She herself had a short grey border, something Vita never copied. She did write of her interest in a "whole series of gardens of restricted colouring" and did insist that their schemes should not exclude a few plants of other tones. However, her detailed plans bear no resemblance to Sissinghurst's in shape or colour. Their plants are much duller; they create a grey garden for August, not a white one for July; they include gold and green gardens, though their orange one is nearer to Sissinghurst's theme for the South Cottage. Miss Jekyll liked "hardy herbaceous flower borders" which the Nicolsons did not. Her range of shrub roses was much narrower than Sissinghurst's.

These authors' books, we might think, were a primary influence. To judge from her library at Sissinghurst, this influence is not at all clear. Like every other keen gardener of the time, Vita had been given Robinson's work, *The English Flower Garden*. I note, however, that her copy of *The Wild Garden* is dated 1938, when Sissinghurst's plan and style were already laid; she did mark his sentences on *Anemone apennina* in grass, an idea which surfaced later in her garden and an *Observer* article. She owned the standard Miss Jekyll on colour schemes and another on annuals and biennials, but neither is marked or very obviously worn and read. Her interest in old roses can only have been stimulated by E.A. Bunyard's *Old Garden Roses*, published in 1936, and by Jason Hill's chapter, *The Rose Revived*, in his *Curious Gardener*, in 1932. Bunyard was a constant mentor for early Sissinghurst problems and we have seen her noting a lavender from Jason Hill's book.

These details do not amount to much. Bunyard's book declared that the old bourbon roses were reduced to four or five varieties, yet these roses, especially, Vita Sackville-West championed and helped to popularize. There were, of course, the gardens at Hidcote Manor in Gloucestershire, but there is no evidence that the Nicolsons visited them in or before Sissinghurst's early days, although she was later to write the Hidcote guide book. For direct inspirations, I think we should look elsewhere, to the verbal advice of friends and the constant enticements of nurserymen's lists and their good descriptions. Her husband's excellent eye and sense of design were there to control and give shape to her plantings. Both, above all, were endebted to their travels and their wide love of literature. Not every garden-maker nowadays is well read, venturing beyond gardening books and lists. Reading and poetry formed a taste, as did the travels which were not just to beaches or a good restaurant. Like the maker of Hidcote, the Nicolsons knew Mediterranean gardens, in Italy, in Constantinople (their first garden, on diplomatic service) and above all, in their early visits to France and Spain which continued to catch Vita's imagination. Lime walks, box, yew, formal designs, good garden pottery, poplars and hornbeam: these are the tastes of European travellers. Some of Vita Sackville-West's best writings concerned places and people in French history: to the old French roses, in particular, she responded. In 1926, she had also visited Persia and appreciated its old forlorn gardens and magnificent wild flowers.

The themes of the garden were not new, neither the herb gardens nor white gardens, the colour planning, the lime tree walk, the bold hedges of yew and the old-fashioned flowers. Yet no border or design was ever copied from a book, no more than the substance of the *Observer* articles. To take one example: in her copy of Patrick Synge's *Plants With Personality*, published in 1939, she marked and noted the pages on the brightly-coloured gerbera, or Barberton daisy, but when she, too, came to write on it for the *Observer*, it was to her own experience that she turned and to the verbal advice of a fellow-gardener. The articles are literary, but not bookish.

Travel and wide reading inclined the Nicolsons to a taste which had restraint and a sense of history: nurserymen's catalogues then fired them with ideas, as did their own early memories and the details which they picked up or transformed from other places and people. The notebooks, again, show Vita responding to the knowledge of friends and contemporaries, but never by slavish imitation. A forgotten link is Colonel Hoare Gray of the nearby Hocker Edge nurseries, who was questioned closely on small plants and bulbs: his pre-war catalogues describe a beguiling range of varieties. Norah and Nancy Lindsay gave valued advice as great plantswomen; so, in response to particular questions, did E.A. Bunyard. The notes for autumn 1937 are accompanied by a careful list of "hybrid musk roses, as described in *Gardening Illustrated*" and almonds, specially recommended in the *Sunday Times*. Comments, however, have been added, sometimes from E.A. Bunyard's advice, then a tick or a red crayon pencil, saying "ordered from Hillings or Hilliers". First, she read; then, she asked specific questions; only then did she order and go her own way when finding a suitable place for the result. "Roses advertised in *Gardeners Chronicle*. 'Phyllis Golden Yellow'. No, Bunyard doesn't recommend". But Bunyard and other friends and growers could only suggest new materials. The questions had to be specific: once, in the notebook, queries for E.A. Bunyard survive. "What fruit trees to plant on the garden wall? About the green fig, can it be bottled ? How to prune peaches? What about fig suckers? Can he recommend a good gardener? Could we graft the pink peach? What about apricots? What about Madresfield Court?".

These questions date from Sissinghurst's early days, but they were not the problems of an innocent beginner. Vita Sackville-West had already made a garden at Long Barn and again, her notebooks survive. In 1916, she was aged 24 and a novice: she thought hepaticas would grow two feet high and suit a windy place and she has to jot down that love-in-a-mist is an annual, to be sown, therefore, in spring. We all begin in this way, but there are already hints of greater interest. Already, she writes romantically of "Italian alkanet", not the botanical name, Anchusa. Already, most unexpectedly, she is planning a garden of pink and mauve flowers only. Elsewhere, she wants orange mimulus, nemesias and orange Iceland poppies, a colour-range which will one day develop in Sissinghurst's cottage garden: the idea of Iceland poppies will re-surface, again in orange, and be mixed with tiger lilies for the Cottage Garden in 1938. Like the poppies, tiger lilies had first been ordered in 1916.

So, surprisingly, had the rose which was to become the most famous of all the many climbers up Sissinghurst's magical brick walls. The blush-white 'Mme Alfred Carrière' flowers with hundreds of buds on the Cottage's south wall. Already in 1916, she had noted "4 'Mme Alfred Carrière', very smelly" for the walls at Long Barn.

These notes are particularly interesting because they precede her visit to Miss Jekyll's great garden in August of the following year. Tiger lilies and orange flowers and this superb rose were favourites of Miss Jekyll too, but Vita did not learn them directly from her visit. Perhaps she had heard of them from friends or read of them in the press; perhaps she had noticed them at her childhood home, Knole, or on one of her outings in high society.

By 1925, she was already thinking of posterity and the future's reactions to her plantings of yew at Long Barn. Already, that year, she and Harold had decided on 215 feet of hornbeam, "32 Irish yews instead of limes", "39 tree-box for dividing up the borders" and 18 cob-nuts. A List of Good Intentions for 1925 begins "plant a Judas tree", and then cancels it with "no, too slow". The strong backbone to their first English garden owed a debt to travels in the Mediterranean where this firm design is common currency in historic gardens. They joined it to the romantic planting which their travels also assisted, gathering seeds casually in other landscapes or seeing flowers in the rough wilderness of Persia: Vita appreciated its lost tradition of rich colour-patterns and evocative types of rose.

At times, Harold Nicolson complained of his wife's romantic attitude to planting and her willingness to jab in any plant when she had space or a spare seedling. He was protesting at particular moments, for the notebooks do bear witness to her constant awareness of the whole, something which he never let slip from their aims. Autumn, 1938, for instance: "remove 'Shot Silk' rose from Cottage Garden (too pink there) and replace by orange-coloured rose now planted alongside 'Ulrich Brunner' in walled garden. Note: this orange rose swears with 'Ulrich Brunner'". Perhaps some plants found their way into Sissinghurst as casual additions, but as Harold Nicolson also recognized, it was not their planter's habit to let her mistakes survive.

These early interests and details could be multiplied but I hope they establish a simple point. Before 1930, the first year of Sissinghurst, let alone winter 1946/7 when the *Observer* articles began, Vita Sackville-West had been noting and gathering, establishing a style and realizing a clearly-formed design. While she later wrote the articles, her husband kept his own notebooks too, exact and detailed, missing no error or failure: each main planting in the Lime Walk is assessed for its virtues or vices and is marked from 1 to 10 to record its peak time of flowering. Sissinghurst was born from these contrasting talents, still visible in the contrasts of the owners' notebooks, and from a long progress which continued and stretched beyond any one decisive 'source'. The Nicolson's gardening was not the work of sudden, fortunate owners of an enchanted site, wondering how to make a garden quickly and looking for a book or an interior designer to tell them how to do it in a socially-approved way.

I would like to illustrate the long, circuitous undergrowth of reading, planning and ideas by two last examples, one from the articles, one from the garden. Once, Vita tells a charming story of Walter Savage Landor and his cook to illustrate a love of violets (page 22 of this book); it is the sort of story most columnists would find to hand in an anthology. In her library of gardening books, I traced it to V. Rendall's forgotten *Wild Flowers In Literature*, where she had marked it in pencil. The book had been sent for review by the *Spectator* in the 1930s; the story had lived for twenty-odd years before it served her in print.

The garden, too, has ideas which surfaced from an earlier phase. No enclosure is more famous or justly admired than the White Garden, at its peak in June and early July. In the last chapter of this book is her own announcement of the plan for its planting in the winter of 1949/50, the "pale garden that I am now planting under the first flakes of snow". Harold Nicolson had proposed it, but it was not a new conception in her mind. She herself had already thought of it in 1939. In the early 1930s she had prefigured her remark about its planting in a curious poem, entitled *The Dream*. She had dreamed she was planting a garden as the night fell in winter, surrounded by burning candles and by fallow deer with flames blazing on their antlers. As she worked, then too, it had been snowing:

> *"And she knew that she neared the end of the garden path*
> *And the deer and the buried candles travelled with her*
> *But still she knew that she would not make an end*
> *Of setting her plants before the shroud came round her . . .".*

The White Garden, which was planted in that snowy winter, still survives to delight its thousands of visitors, just as these articles, despite their author's distaste for them, have delighted thousands of readers, whether gardeners or garden-watchers.

*J*ANUARY

Hear next of winter, when the florid summer,
The bright barbarian scarfed in a swathe of flowers,
The corn a golden earring on her cheek,
Has left our north to winter's finer etching,
To raw-boned winter, when the sun
Slinks in a narrow and a furtive arc,
Red as the harvest moon, from east to west,
And the swans go home at dusk to the leaden lake
Dark in the plains of snow.

Water alone remains untouched by snow.

The Land

*M*YSTERIOUS SCENTS

It might be agreeable to start the year with a consideration of scents, a mysterious and alluring subject suggested to me by the queer behaviour of two pots of Persian cyclamen I had raised from seed of a specially selected sweet-scented strain. They smelt delicious in the greenhouse and I carried them triumphantly indoors. All trace of scent disappeared, but that might be attributed to the change of temperature, or moisture in the air, and even a relative lack of light. Two days later, however, the whole room was fragrant, but, mark this, the fragrance emanated from only one of the two pots. Next day the situation was reversed: the plant that had been scentless was now doing all that could be wished of it, and the other wasn't.

So it has gone on. Identical twins could not be living under more identical conditions, yet they continue to choose different days and different hours of the day for their performance. Why?

We know that we owe our pleasure in flower-scent to certain essential oils. They are contained in cells which release their content by some process not fully understood. The essential oils are what we call attars, one of the few words for which the English language has to thank the Persian. (Attar of roses will be the most familiar to most people.) The chemical composition of these attars has been analysed, and you would be surprised to learn what everyday substances we should encounter if we were to take some favourite petals to pieces, alcohol for instance, vinegar, benzine; but I am no chemist and should blunder into some shocking howlers were I to pursue the subject. I profess to be nothing more than the average gardener, enjoying such useless but charming bits of information as that some

A view of the moat and the summer house on an icy winter day.

butterflies and moths exude the same scent as the flowers they visit; that white flowers are the most numerous among the scented kinds, followed by red, yellow, and purple in that order, with blue a very bad fifth; that flowers fertilised by birds have no scent at all, birds being without a sense of smell; that dark-haired people have the most highly developed sense, whereas albinos are generally lacking it altogether; that some flowers smell different in the morning from in the evening; and, finally, that the flower-like scent so often observed emanating from the dead bodies of saintly persons may be due to the same breaking-down or release of essential oils in the first stages of decomposition. This supposedly mystical fragrance is usually said to suggest roses or violets.

None of all this, however, explains the peculiar conduct of my two cyclamen.

*B*Y THE WATERSIDE
Oh! what fun I have been having with a plant token given me for Christmas for two whole guineas.

Two whole guineas. What a wealth of potential beauty it conjures up. What shall we order?

I came to the conclusion that the most satisfactory way to deal with a plant token was to concentrate its value on some definite form of plan. You might need plants for the herbaceous border, or you might need roses, or you might need plants for the rock garden, or you might need herbs for the herb garden or shrubs for the mixed border or bulbs for the spring garden. Whichever it is, one's gratitude to the donor is more likely to survive than if it were dissipated in unrelated plants dotted about all over the place. Always assuming, of course, that the plants themselves survive.

My own choice was for the waterside. The pickerel weed, or *Pontederia cordata*, is a North American which likes to grow in six or more inches of water and should rapidly increase to a good clump from its creeping root stock. Bright blue in summer, standing two foot high, it looks proud and effective.

Then there is *Sagittaria*, well-named arrowhead from the shape of its leaves, with flowers of white and gold, not unlike the familiar Christmas rose. *Sagittaria sagittifolia* is a native of Britain and thus should be the most reliable, but there is also a double form of it, if you like double forms, which I don't, called 'Flore Pleno' which I think comes from Japan. Don't plant the variety called *latifolia* if you happen to have carp in your pond. They will eat it.

Finally, I come to the flowering rush, *Butomus umbellatus*. This is also a native plant, but it doesn't look like one. It looks more like something exquisitely drawn in the foreground of a Persian miniature. It has such elegance of design and such delicacy of rose-pink colour, that you could scarcely believe it originated anywhere nearer home than Central Asia. It does in fact occur in Asia also, where, regrettably, the local population is reported as eating the root stocks, much as the Japanese used to eat the bulbs of *Lilium auratum* growing wild on the slopes of Fujiyama before they discovered their value in the European market. However, the flowering rush has its own way of defending itself: the leaves are said to be so sharp as to wound the mouths of animals attempting to browse upon them.

I lost every single one of this little collection of water-plants years ago, not because they were not all perfectly hardy, but because I made the mistake of combining them with ornamental ducks. I thought the ducks would clear the water of duckweed, as indeed they did, but they also cleared it of all my lovely blue and pink and white inflorescence. This time I shall surround each clump with mesh-wire.

*P*LANT ASSOCIATIONS

Plant associations provide one of the most fascinating and amusing side-lines in the formation of any garden. Perhaps side-line is the wrong word, for as the designer's ambitions burgeon so does he realise the importance of this element in the creation of his picture, and what is a garden, in the last resort, but the creation of a picture or a series of pictures? The fun of this aspect of gardening is that it adapts itself to any scale, from the grandiose to the tiny. You get the great gardens such as Bodnant or Stourhead, so large as to form part of the landscape; you get the diminutive rock garden where a little fringed dianthus may share a pocket with a dwarf primula in perfect fragment of composition.

Sometimes one picks up ideas on holidays abroad when one may see the native flora disposing itself in its own chosen way. No way is better, as all walkers over the high Alpine pastures will agree. I recall especially, on this northern January morning, a pine-scented wood in the Dolomites in June where *Clematis alpina* had twisted its growth upwards through some scrubby trees and hung its pale lilac heads high above the martagon lilies growing in the leafy soil beneath. It made such a natural picture, so right, so suitable, so ordained. I thought then, and I think now, that one might reproduce that arrangement in a corner of one's own garden.

I envisage a raised bank, ideally supported by a low wall. On the top of this bank or shelf, which would give good drainage, you plant rosemary or lavender. Having planted your top shelf with rosemary or lavender, you then plant *Clematis alpina,* sometimes called *Atragene alpina,* amongst the bushes and let it ramble horizontally all through them.

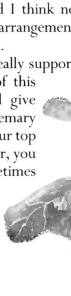

Cyclamen persicum

You also put in some bulbs of *Lilium martagon*, which will enjoy the protection of the rosemary or lavender, and is one of the easiest lilies to grow, and should reappear happily year after year and even increase; it is said that *Lilium martagon* has naturalised itself in some parts of this country. This is an encouraging bit of news for some of us who find lilies difficult and disappointing.

It is a good plan to place an inverted ridge-tile over the roots of clematis, as a protection against any breaking of the fibrous roots when forking the bed. So easily done, so fatal in its results. But remember that slugs love hiding-places such as inverted ridge-tiles, and also love the young shoots of clematis, so put down some slug-bait at the same time.

ARTFUL DISORDER

A Chinese gardener once observed to Sir William Chambers that as our clothes are artificial, so must a garden differ likewise from the vulgar simplicity of nature. This remark gives one to ponder. To what extent does one want one's garden trim and tidy?

Opinions seem to differ. Some people are so madly wild-flower minded as to encourage such invasive things as celandine, which one must agree looks extremely pretty with its varnished golden face in the right place, on a bank under a hedgerow for instance, but not as a plant smothering more precious things in one's garden.

Then there are dead-nettles. You have to be a very highbrow gardener indeed to like dead-nettles. Personally I prefer every nettle of every kind dead and eradicated, but then I must confess to a preference for keeping my garden weedless and tidy.

It isn't that I don't like a sweet disorder, but it has to be judiciously arranged. I like things to toss about freely, if such is their nature, but I do also like to see the underneath flawlessly neat and clean. I like to see young trees clear of grass at their roots, giving them a chance to receive rain. I like to see the verges of lawns sharply cut, because a lawn demands a strict formality. I don't like to see ground-elder poking up its ugly leaf amongst irises, its favourite domicile, knowing by some devilish instinct how hard it is going to be to dig it out. I don't like coltsfoot, with leaves as large as soup-plates. I don't like bindweed, with long tapeworm roots going down deeper than one's eventual grave. And I really hate groundsel, a hideous little vulgarian for whom the only good thing to be said is that it can be so easily suppressed at birth.

There are, however, some wild plants which I encourage in my garden. The wild violets, so rightly called *odorata*, purple or white, I love so much that I can almost enter into the feelings of Walter Savage Landor, that man of intractable temper, who having thrown his cook out of the window exclaimed "Good God! I forgot the violets".

Viola odorata

Then there are the wood anemones, especially when one has the luck to find a pink sort growing in local woods. Please do not imagine me as a vandal recklessly digging up wild flowers and transplanting them with no chance of survival. I hope I know better than that, and may even claim to have saved some beauties from extermination. I would not dare to lift a Bee Orchid from its native chalk, and would pray only that no picnicker should come along and take a fancy to it.

To sum up, what have I said? That I like a tidy garden innocent of ugly or invasive weeds. That I am all in favour of introducing some of our native plants so long as we know they will flourish and may be rescued from the depredation of ploughing or that even worse depredation of weed-killer sprayed along our road-verges.

*H*OW TO ENLIVEN PRIVET
A reader wants suggestions about how to enliven a "flat, dull privet hedge", and I dare say that there are a good many people who would be glad to transform an uninteresting hedge into a thing of comparative beauty. There is no inherent difficulty so long as you bear two facts in mind. The first is that every hedge, privet or otherwise, is a robber of the soil; its intricate web of roots demands sustenance and moisture, with consequent deprivation of any competing occupants.

The moral is obvious: you must feed as richly as possible by top-dressings of whatever good food you can acquire, whether it be organic or inorganic manuring, to compensate the plunder and pillage and spoliation going on all the time beneath the ground. The second fact is that your hedge will have to be clipped annually, and clipped severely; therefore you must choose your ramblers and climbers from the category of plants which do not mind being chopped about by shears, possibly at quite the wrong time of year.

After all this cautionary preamble I shall be expected to suggest some real toughs. I think I would plant *Clematis montana*, either the ordinary white kind or its pale pink variety 'Rubens'. This seems to survive any cruelty. Then I would have wisteria, either the ordinary mauve or the more exquisite white, both such strong growers that although they would not get any very expert pruning or spurring back but would just get slaughtered in a way to make any professional gardener scream in his sleep, would still prosper and perhaps be all the better for it. Then I would have some of the autumn-colouring vines, the magnificent huge-leaved *Vitis coignetiae*, for instance, bright pink in September; or *Vitis vinifera* 'Brandt', carrying bunches of small black grapes; and I should certainly have two or three of the twining *Celastrus orbiculatus*, which isn't much to look at during the summer but which surprises us with its red-and-yellow clusters of fruit in October, and is invaluable for picking as it lasts for weeks and weeks indoors.

The disadvantage of the vines and the celastrus would be the necessity of leaving the hedge-clipping till rather late in the year, but I can't see why one should be tied to the calendar for clipping such nasty hedges as privet. They are indestructible whatever you do, short of taking a bulldozer to root them out, so why not leave them until later than the orthodox date? I am all for playing rough with things that play rough with us, and for making them behave as our servants, not our masters. And so

Chimonanthus praecox

I think that if you are afflicted with a flat, dull hedge you should take no notice at all of the time of year the books tell you to cut it, but should regard it merely as a host to the lovelier guests you wish to weave through it.

HOW TO PRUNE WINTER SWEET

The pruning of that most deliciously scented shrub, the winter sweet, *Chimonanthus praecox*, has worried me for many years, as I daresay it has worried other amateur gardeners who are wise enough to grow it. The advice we are given by the experts does not seem to work in practice. The experts all agree that the winter sweet grown as a bush in the open demands no pruning at all, but as most of us grow it trained against a wall let me quote what some of the authorities have to say about that:

> Prune back the flowered shoots close to the main stem immediately after flowering, so as to encourage the new summer's growth on which next winter's flowers will be borne.
>
> W. Arnold Forster, *Shrubs for the Milder Counties*

> On wall-plants the older wood should be cut after flowering to encourage new growth.
>
> Patrick Synge, *Flowers in Winter*

> They should be pruned directly after flowering: the growths that have flowered should be cut clean out to encourage the formation of new wood, for it is from this that the winter blossoms are produced.
>
> A.W. Darnell, *Winter Blossoms from the Outdoor Garden*

And, finally, the great Mr Bean himself, whose four volumes on *Trees and Shrubs Hardy in the British Isles* is the Bible of all tree and shrub growers, tells us not to defer pruning much beyond February, so that the fullest possible length of time is allowed for the new growths to be made on which depend the next winter's crop of flowers.

Now I obediently followed all these instructions, which in the main suggested that we should chop hard back to the old wood in February. I cut back all the bits that had flowered, as I was told to do, and what happened? I got long young shoots, healthy as could be, but with never a promise of a flower on them. This was the young growth on which I was told to depend for this winter's crop of flowers. But now observation persuades me that these young shoots will flower in January two years hence, not in January next year, and that the solution is to have two plants, flowering alternate years. Staggered, in fact.

*P*UZZLING PUYAS

Many years ago Mr Clarence Elliott found an aloe-like plant growing in an extremely localised patch on the slopes of the Chilean Andes, and introduced it to England under the name *Puya alpestris*. He very generously gave me two seedlings at the time, which have thriven and flower about once in seven years.

The flower is worth waiting for. It rises on a straight stem out of its wickedly spiny rosette of leaves, to a height of about two feet, and it carries its strange, metallic blossoms of peacock-blue and orange all the way up the stem. They look as though they were made of painted tin rather than of the soft texture of a flower.

Interposed at intervals among these beautiful though somewhat nightmarish blossoms are horizontal brown spikes, some six inches long and tapering to a point, manifestly placed there for some utilitarian purpose. Mr Elliott told me he understood them to be intended as perches for the humming-birds searching the depths of the flowers for nectar.

This sounded romantic enough, but I had always held some reservation of conviction in my mind. Had I not been brought up to believe that humming-birds fed while on the wing, darting rapidly at the flower even as our own familiar hawkmoth darts? Yet I was reluctant to give up the association between the puya and its tiny feathered compatriot.

Now that I am myself on the way to Chile, I believe I may have hit on the solution. I offer it humbly, as it may by now be perfectly well known to Mr Elliott and to all who grow or take an interest in the puya. It was suggested to me by a fellow-traveller, an expert on the birds of South America. Confirming my supposition that humming-birds fed while in flight, he added the information that humming-birds, like our native robin, are exceedingly pugnacious little creatures, and like to settle on some post of vantage to survey the surrounding territory. Could this, he asked, be the purpose of the puya's perches? Sated with nectar, you take a rest while looking about for any possible enemy.

It sounds plausible.

I am writing far from any notes or books of reference, and cannot for the moment remember the adjectival name of a puya I once saw from Tresco in Sicily. A terrifying plant, it towered to a height of at least six feet and put *alpestris* completely into the shade. Whether it grows in the open at Tresco I am unable to say, but I should strongly advise any visitor to that famous garden to look out for it, not that it would be easy to miss. When I saw it, it was in a pot at a flower show in Cornwall, and speaking from memory the month was April, so that would be approximately the time to seek for it. With me, in the colder climate of Kent, *P. alpestris* when it condescends to flower at all does so towards the middle of May. Goodness knows what it does in Chile.

SWEETBRIAR HEDGES

Someone has been pleading with me to put in a good word for sweetbriar. I do so most willingly, for a hedge of sweetbriar is one of the most desirable things in any garden.

It is thorny enough to keep out intruders, should it be needed as a boundary protection; in early summer it is as pretty as the dog rose, with its pale pink single flowers; in autumn it turns itself into a sheer wall of scarlet hips, and on moist muggy evenings after rain at any time of the year the scent is really and truly strong in the ambient air. You do not need to crush a leaf between your fingers to provoke the scent: it swells out towards you of its own accord, as you walk past, like a great sail filling suddenly with a breeze off those Spice Islands which Columbus hoped to find.

These are many virtues to claim, but even so we may add to them. It is the Eglantine of the poets, if you like that touch of romance. True, Milton seems to have confused it with something else, probably the honeysuckle:

> . . . *Through the sweetbriar or the vine,*
> *Or the twisted eglantine . . .*

but what does that matter? it is pedantic to be so precise, and we should do better to take a hint from Milton and plant a *mixed* hedge of honeysuckle and sweetbriar, with perhaps an ornamental vine twining amongst them – the purple-leafed vine, *Vitis vinifera* 'Purpurea', would look sumptuous among the red hips in October.

I have never seen a hedge of this composition; but why not? Ideas come to one; and it remains only to put them into practice. The nearest that I have got is to grow the common *Clematis jackmanii* into my sweetbriar, planting the clematis on the north side of the hedge, where the roots are cool and shaded and the great purple flowers come wriggling through southwards into the sun. It looks fine, and the briar gives the clematis just the twiggy kind of support it needs.

Sweetbriar is a strong grower, but is often blamed for going thin and scraggy towards the roots. I find that you can correct this disadvantage by planting your hedge in the first instance against a system of post-and-wire, and subsequently tying-in the long shoots to the posts and wire instead of pruning them. Tie the shoots horizontally, or bend them downwards if need be, thus obtaining a thick dense growth, which well compensates you for the initial trouble of setting up the posts and wire. They will last for years, and so will the briar.

The common sweetbriar will spread, horizontally, twenty feet or more. The Penzance hybrid briars are more expensive, but 'Amy Robsart', with deep rose flowers, and 'Lady Penzance', with coppery-yellow flowers, are particularly to be recommended.

AMONG THE CATALOGUES

January is a dead season, when one cannot get out to do anything active in the garden, so one is reduced to studying catalogues under the lamp and thereby being induced to order far more plants or seeds than one ought to.

I have ordered a summer-flowering tamarisk, *Tamarix pentandra*. This will flower in August, I hope, during that dull heavy month when flowering shrubs are few. We do not grow the tamarisks enough; they are so graceful, so light and buoyant, so feathery, so pretty when smothered in their rose-pink flower. The earlier-flowering one is *Tamarix tetrandra*; it comes out in April to May.

The seed catalogues are my undoing. I have grown wise, after many years of gardening, and no longer order recklessly from wildly alluring descriptions which make every annual sound easy to grow and as brilliant as a film star. I now know that gardening is not like that. Yet I can still be decoyed into ordering some packets of the Roggli pansies and the Chabaud carnations, having learnt from experience how good and repaying they are. The pansies, if sown in March under glass, will scarcely flower this summer, or at any rate not until September, but by next year they should have made fine clumps which will start flowering in May and should continue without remission until the first autumn frosts. The annual carnations, however, if sown in February under glass (a seed box in a frame or under a hand-light) should fill bare patches this summer and are as pretty and scented as anyone could desire. They can be had in self-colours, or flaked and striped like the pinks in old flower-paintings; with their old-

Clematis jackmanii and *Rosa* 'Amy Robsart'

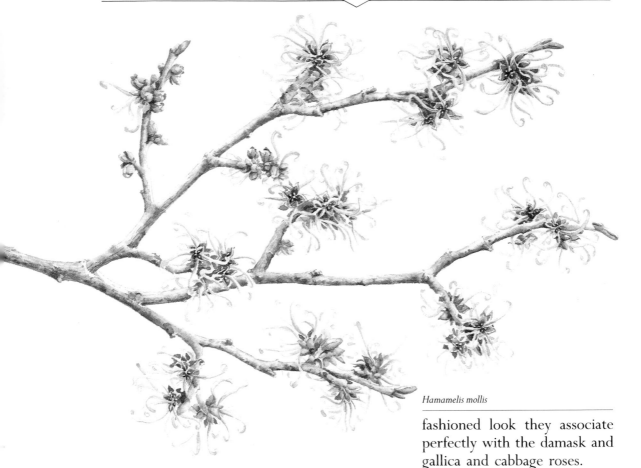

Hamamelis mollis

fashioned look they associate perfectly with the damask and gallica and cabbage roses.

"Carnation" is perhaps a misleading term, since to most people, myself included, carnation suggests a greenhouse plant of the Malmaison type: an expensive buttonhole for a dandy at Ascot or Lord's. The Chabaud carnations are more like what we think of as our grandmother's pinks. Please make a point of getting the two strains I have recommended: the Roggli pansies, and the Chabaud carnations. They are by far the best I know.

*S*TRANGELY NEGLECTED WITCH HAZEL

When the early settlers first found themselves self-exiled in that wild and dangerous territory of North America now known to their descendants as Virginia, they discovered in the thickets and undergrowth a shrubby thing that reminded them of the common old hazel they had known in England. They took the forked twigs and used them for dowsing or water-divining, as they had used hazel-twigs at home. This was *Hamamelis virginiana*, and they called it the witch hazel, because any twig that would twitch in the hand must necessarily have something to do with a witch or a wizard. A pleasing derivation, but our own hazel has no botanical connection with *Hamamelis*, and much as we may appreciate its catkins in spring and the squirrels its nuts in autumn, we must not allow ourselves to be misled.

The witch hazels we now grow in our gardens are far better than the one our forefathers found in Virginia. *Hamamelis virginiana* is a very poor thing compared with the Chinese *Hamamelis mollis* or the Japanese *Hamamelis japonica* 'Arborea'. These have both been coming into their full beauty since Twelfth Night. They are queer-looking plants, with their twisted growth and their twisted ribbons of flower. One always regrets not having planted more of a thing one likes. This may not be good English, but it is good gardening advice. If I could go back twenty years, I should plant a whole little grove of the two Asiatics and should now have many large bushes to chop from, instead of being stingy about the few twigs I spare to give my friends. The witch hazel does not lend itself happily to cutting, which is a pity, for it is ideal as a picked flower, very long-lasting, decorative, and capable of scenting a whole room. But it never seems to break out again, as most flowering shrubs do, so when you cut you spoil the chance of next year's shoot. This is the sort of warning that books never give. One has to find out for oneself.

Apart from this drawback there could be no more accommodating shrub. It may be rather slow of development, but it will start to flower quite young, and will accept any reasonable soil, preferably of a loamy nature. It likes sunlight, to ripen its wood, but will stand up to cold winds even from the north and east, and its flowers are extraordinarily frost-resistant. On winter mornings you can see the crinkled gold coming through the rime like sugared crystallised fruits. If I add to this that in the autumn the leaves turn as yellow as a quince, perhaps I shall have said enough to encourage a wider use of this strangely neglected treasure.

EBRUARY

In February, if the days be clear,
The waking bee, still drowsy on the wing,
Will guess the opening of another year
And blunder out to seek another spring.
Crashing through winter sunlight's pallid gold,
His clumsiness sets catkins on the willow
Ashake like lambs' tails in the early fold,
Dusting with pollen all his brown and yellow,
But when the rimy afternoon turns cold
And undern squalls buffet the chilly fellow,
He'll seek the hive's warm waxen welcoming
And set about the chambers' classic mould.

The Land

CARING FOR CYCLAMEN

This is the time of year when people begin to get worried about their pots of cyclamen and how to treat them in the ensuing months. I suppose that everybody knows they ought to be allowed to dry off gradually and not be started into life again until next July or August, but as I was talking the other day to a big commercial grower I thought I might pass on a few of the hints he gave me.

He advised sinking the pots out of doors in a shady place into a bed of peat or ashes, up to the rim. This, he said, would retain just the right amount of moisture without any need for watering throughout the months when the corm needs to rest.

He does not advise keeping the same corm for more than two or three years. He says that at the end of that time the quality of the flowers begins to deteriorate, although a second-year corm should produce a larger quantity of flower than a first-year corm. I should not mind the diminished size, myself, since whopping ogreish flowers hold no especial charm for me, but that is a matter of taste. He recommends sowing seeds in seed-boxes in June, which means that the little plants will have reached flowering-size in eighteen months, i.e., seeds sown in June should flower by Christmas next year. Of course it also means having a warm greenhouse in which to winter them, and not everybody can boast of that. I daresy that some very green-fingered persons could raise them on a window sill in a permanently warm kitchen. It is certainly the most economical way of ensuring a staggered supply, if you can manage it.

My good friend, the commercial grower, who, like most true gardeners, is very willing to impart his knowledge, gave me some further tips. Never, he said, pull a

Crocus tomasinianus growing in the lawn in front of a yew hedge.

yellowed leaf away. In so doing you may strip off a bit of the skin of the corm, and thus do damage. Cut it off with a knife. Don't tug. On the other hand, always pull the flower stalk away vertically should you want to detach it from the corm. I did know that much, though the bit about the leaf was new to me. How ignorant one is, and how much one learns in ten minutes' talk with an expert!

But wise and expert though he is, he has not been able to resolve a question I asked him. Why do some pots of cyclamen go off suddenly, looking miserable and moribund after two days indoors, when other pots kept in exactly the same conditions survive healthily after weeks indoors? He could not answer my query. He just stood surveying his enormous cathedral, roofed by glass and carpeted by thousands of cyclamen, rose-red, cherry-red, shell-pink, orchid-mauve, blood-red, virginal-white, all as healthy as could be, and gave me a pitying smile.

CHABAUD CARNATIONS AGAIN

In response to so many requests, I wish to return to the subject of Chabaud carnations. M. Chabaud was a botanist from Toulon who, in about 1870, raised this hybrid between the old perennial carnation and annual kind.

There are two sorts, the annual and the perennial. The annuals are divided into the 'Giant Chabaud', the 'Enfant de Nice', and the 'Compact Dwarf'. They should be sown in February or March in boxes of well-mixed leaf mould, soil, and sharp sand. They require no heat; but in frosty weather the seedlings should be protected. Do not over-water. Keep them on the dry side. Plant them out when they are large enough, in a sunny place with good drainage. (I think myself that they look best in a bed by themselves, not mixed in with other plants.) Their colour range is wide: yellow, white, red, purple, pink, and striped. They are extremely prolific, and if sown now should be in flower from July onwards. If you care to take the trouble, they can be lifted in October and potted, to continue flowering under glass or indoors on a window-sill, that is, safely away from frost, well into the winter.

The perennial sort, which is perfectly hardy, should be sown March-June and planted out this summer to flower during many summers to come. Those gardeners who appreciate a touch of historical tradition will be gratified to know that in the variety called 'Flammand' they are getting a seventeenth-century strain and may expect the flaked and mottled flower so often seen in those enchanting muddles crammed into an urn in Dutch flower paintings. Indeed, the catalogue of these seeds is full of romance, not only historical but geographical, if you agree with me that there is something romantic in the thought of Provence, from which your seeds will come. Have you been to St Remy, that Roman settlement in what was once South-eastern Gaul, where a Roman triumphal arch still stands, and where flowers are now grown in mile-wide stretches for the seed market? It must be a wonderful sight, when all the carnations and zinnias and petunias are in flower, staining the blistered landscape of Van Gogh's Provence in acres of colour.

This is perhaps neither here nor there in an article on practical gardening, but I always get led away in excitement over the plants I recommend. I was led away also by a note in the same catalogue about petunias, a special strain grown by the nuns in a convent near Toulon. I have not tried these yet, but I mean to. I like thinking about those Sisters in Toulon, pottering about their convent garden, saving their petunia seeds, and sending them to us in England for our delight.

GLADIOLI UNDER GLASS

That frail and lovely little *Gladiolus colvillei* 'The Bride' should have been potted up before Christmas, but it is not too late to do so now. If I had a stony, sun-baked terrace on the Riviera I should grow it by the hundred; as it is, I content myself with a dozen in two pots under glass. I know very well that people do grow it out of doors in England, lifting the corms each autumn as you would do with other gladioli, but its white delicacy is seen to better advantage as a picked flower than lost in the competition of the garden.

Some gardeners have a theory that the corms are not worth keeping after the first year and that it is better to renew annually. I believe this to be an unnecessarily extravagant idea. The little offsets always to be found clustering round the parent corm may be grown on until they come to flowering size in their second year. Naturally, this means a preliminary gap of one season, but once the rhythm is established the succession is assured. I have found that the same system works with *Acidanthera bicolor murielae*, itself a form of gladiolus, and with those tiny starry narcissi *watereri*, which are difficult to keep otherwise and rather expensive to buy. These, by the way, are a real treasure for a pan in an alpine house or in a raised trough out of doors where they can be examined at leisure and more or less at eye level.

An easier treasure on a staging under glass is the winter aconite. I somewhat nervously lifted a few clumps from the garden just as they were beginning to hump themselves in their round-shouldered way through the ground before the snow came, and transferred them with a fat ball of soil into a couple of low pans. They do not seem to have minded in the least, and are flowering like little suns, a bright sight on a winter morning. It is remarkable how frost-resistant their soft petals are. There is no heating in that greenhouse, and the pans are frozen solid, yet the golden petals remain untouched and I know that when the snow has cleared away, their garden companions will flourish regardless of how many degrees of frost may follow the disappearance of the warm white blanket.

Eranthis hyemalis

TABLOID GARDENING

I am not at all sure that I approve of tabloid gardening. I like to think of old gardeners pottering their life-time away in green baize aprons, straw hats, a twist of raffia behind their ears, and a Nannie-like intimacy with the plants under their care. Nowadays people prefer things to be made easy for them, perhaps because modern life is too busy and intricate for specialisation, and so we get book societies telling us what we ought to read, and nurserymen's catalogues telling us what we ought to plant.

It does save trouble, and I suppose must be tolerated as a symptom. For the bewildered novice it is certainly convenient to be offered what are described as Collections: they range from the Best Border Perennials to the Best Plants for Crazy Paving. You will note that they are usually called The Best. This does not necessarily mean the most choice, but it does generally mean the most reliable. I quote from one catalogue, proposing a Rock Garden Collection: "All are good hearty growers with no special fads or fancies ... free flowering and of bright showy colours ... selected, so far as is possible, to give a succession of flower from Spring to Autumn. We feel confident that this Collection will give pleasure to those who want an effective display without a lot of fuss and trouble". No doubt it will and, moreover, you know exactly what you are going to spend, from thirty-six plants at £3 7s. 6d. to 180 plants at £13 10s. I don't like it; it goes against every grain of my make-up; what I enjoy doing is to make a success of something rather difficult to manage; yet why should I try to impose my own quirks on the readers of these articles? The beginner must be considered as well as the connoisseur. Gardening is terribly confusing at the start (and even at the end, believe me). There seem to be such myriads of plants, all equally desirable, all so tempting to order, all setting out with such promise as one unwraps them from their strawy bundles or unpacks them from their little pots, all so heart-breakingly liable to disappear before they have completed one year of life. Infant mortality in the Middle Ages is the only approximate comparison. It is to the beginner who wants a short-cut to his objective that I commend a study of the Collections listed in these caressive catalogues.

CROCUSES IN BOWLS

Children have a gift for asking apparently simple questions to which there is no real answer. I was asked: "What is your favourite flower?" The reply seemed almost

Crocus imperati and *C. chrysanthus*

to suggest itself: "Any flower, turn by turn, which happens to be in season at the moment".

Thus, I now find myself regretting that I did not plant more of the species crocuses which are busy coming out in quick succession. They are so very charming, and so very small. Grown in bowls or alpine pans they are enchanting for the house; they recall those miniature works of art created by the great Russian artificer Fabergé in the luxurious days when the very rich could afford such extravagances. Grown in stone troughs out of doors, they look exquisitely in scale with their surroundings, since in open beds or even in pockets of a rockery they are apt to get lost in the vast areas of landscape beyond. One wants to see them close to the eye, fully to appreciate the pencilling on the outside of the petals; it seems to have been drawn with a fine brush, perhaps wielded by some sure-handed Chinese calligrapher, feathering them in bronze or in lilac. Not the least charm of these little crocuses is their habit of throwing up several blooms to a stem (it is claimed for *ancyrensis* that a score will grow from a single bulb). Just when you think they are going off, a fresh crop appears.

Crocus ancyrensis, from Ankara and Asia Minor, yellow, is usually the first to flower in January or early February, closely followed by *chrysanthus* and its varieties 'E.A.Bowles', yellow and brown; 'E.P.Bowles', a deeper yellow feathered with purple; 'Moonlight', sulphur-yellow and cream; 'Snow Bunting', cream and lilac; 'Warley White', feathered with purple. That fine species, *C.imperati*, from Naples and Calabria, is slightly larger, violet-blue and straw-coloured; it flowers in February. *C.susianus*, February and March, is well known as the Cloth of Gold crocus; *sieberi*, a Greek, lilac-blue, is also well known; but *suterianus* and its variety 'Jamie' are less often seen. 'Jamie' must be the tiniest of all: a pale violet with deeper markings on the outside, it is no more than an inch across when fully expanded, and two inches high. I measured. I have mentioned only a few of this delightful family, which should, by the way, be planted in August.

*F*UN FOR THE SHUT-IN
    A letter from America reminds me that people who wish to grow the ornamental gourds this summer should order the seeds now. Most of the big seedsmen stock them, and they can be had in a variety of shapes and colours, from the great orange pumpkins (*potirons*), so familiar a sight as they lie hugely about in the fields of France, to the little striped white-and-green, no larger than a tennis ball. They should be grown under the same conditions as the vegetable marrow; picked when ripe; and lightly varnished to preserve them for indoor amusement throughout the winter.

It appears that there is a Gourd Society in North Carolina. Our American friends never do things by halves; and although their fondness for a tricksy ingenuity may sometimes outrun ours, I thought I might pass on some of their ideas for the benefit of those who have the leisure and the inclination to carry them out. Thus the elongated Dutchman's pipe gourd may be scooped out and transformed into a ladle. The circular, medium-sized kinds may be scooped out likewise and turned into bowls. A pleasant occupation for an invalid, possibly – what an extract from an American catalogue calls "Fun for the shut-in".

The supreme example of North Carolinan ingenuity comes from one competitor in the Society's exhibition. She had turned a vast pumpkin into a coach for Cinderella, drawn by eight mouse-sized gourds. What a hint for our Women's Institutes, at their Autumn Produce Show, in this Coronation year!

More pleasing to our taste, perhaps, is the harvest festival the Gourd Society organises for the thousands of people who flock to see it. Throughout the summer, members of the Society have grown ornamental grasses to mix with their gourds; and this reminds me that I had always wanted to grow a patch of *Phalaris canariensis*, in plain English, canary seed, in my garden, partly for fun, partly because I could then give a dollop of seed to any friend who kept a canary, and partly and principally because this form of shakers or quaking grass was called in the first Elizabethan reign, when writers had some sense of vivid naming, the Petty Panick.

ROUND THE PORCH

A lady writes to say she has an ugly porch to her house, and what evergreen climber can she grow to cover it up? Her hope is to obscure the porch all the year round. No doubt many people find themselves in a similar predicament, so a note on the subject may be useful. The trouble is that few climbers, with the exception of ivy, are evergreen; and that those which are, tend to be only half-hardy. Amongst true climbers I can think of two honeysuckles, *Lonicera giraldii* and *L.henryi*; one of each, planted either side of the porch, should soon grow up to intertwine overhead. But this does not take us very far, and it becomes necessary to look round for some substitutes.

We may find them amongst the tall-growing shrubs which can be treated as a kind of buttress or side-piers, and induced by means of wire to grow horizontally across the top. *Ceanothus rigidus* and *Ceanothus thyrsiflorus* both come to mind, with dark green leaves and powder-blue flowers; reasonably hardy, they will attain a height of twelve and thirty feet respectively. They could not, however, look so tidy as something which could be clipped into shape; and that makes me think of the sweet bay, *Laurus nobilis*. You know how sometimes, on old country cottages, one sees a kind of deep, dense porch, generally cut out of yew or box, giving an air of solidity and mystery to the entrance, which would be especially welcome in a brand-new, perhaps rather insubstantial, dwelling. There is no reason why the sweet bay, with its aromatic foliage, should not

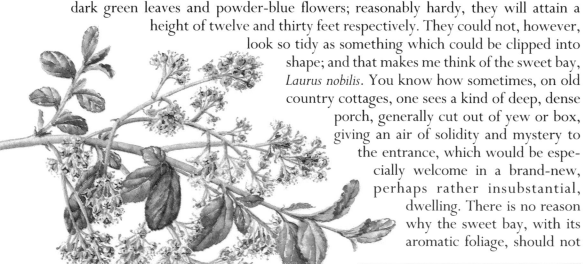

Ceanothus thyrsiflorus

be used for a similar purpose, to frame and disguise the objectionable porch. It is of fairly rapid growth, and will put up with any amount of shaping. Within a few years, it should provide the front-door with a dark-green cavern of shelter.

If my correspondent thinks this sounds gloomy, though personally I think that a bit of gloom is of immense value in a garden, as a foil to the bright flowers, she might try planting two of the pop-lar-like cherries as senti-nels either side of her porch. True, they are not evergreen, but their mass of pale pink blossom is a delight of youthfulness in spring. *Prunus amanogawa* is the name, meaning Celestial River, the Japanese equivalent of our Milky Way.

May I thank all those enviable people who have written to say that their passion-flower does produce its fruits in their gardens? Mostly West country gardens, I may add, though there was one triumphant letter from Hampshire, which is not so very far west.

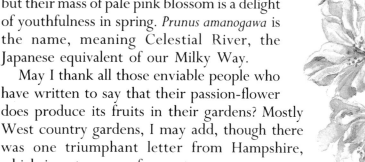

Prunus amanogawa

BASHFUL ANNUALS

Annuals for sunny places are for the most part so well known and so widely grown that it would be almost an insult to list them, and a waste of space to remind you of such things as clarkia, alyssum, candytuft, eschscholzia, petunia, or even nemesia, which certainly gives the highest value for brilliance of colour.

It might therefore be more useful if I were to single out a few which, although quite as easy to grow, seem to have remained oddly bashful with a dislike of publicity. I never tire of recommending *Phacelia campanularia*, and never cease to be surprised when visitors to my garden ask me what it is. Try it. Sow it at intervals of a fortnight from April onwards; put down slug-bait; thin it out to six inches apart; and then see what you think of it. Sheets of blue.

Then there are the South Africans; venidium, ursinia, dimorphotheca, all in the range of yellow to orange; and if you want to increase the orange touch on the palette of your border, there is *Cosmos* 'Orange Ruffles', three-foot tall, feathery of leaf, starry of flower, long-lasting, and pretty enough in a mixed bunch to please even Mrs Constance Spry.

At the foot of all these yellow-to-orange things, you might sow a vast patch of *Limnanthes douglasii*, beloved of bees, and more descriptively known as the poached egg flower. I should not have called it poached egg myself: I should have called it scrambled egg with chopped parsley; poached suggests something far more circular and cohesive. I know this is a very ordinary annual to recommend, but one does so easily forget old favourites that a reminder may be forgiven.

Looking back on what I have just written, I see I said sow a vast patch. I am sure this is good and sound advice. Always exaggerate rather than stint. Masses are more effective than mingies.

I have long since abandoned the practice of sowing zinnias in seed-boxes, and I do believe that you get sturdier plants in the long run, when the seedlings have suffered no disturbance. Sow the seeds in little parties of three or four, and thin them remorselessly when they are about two inches high, till only one lonely seedling remains. It will do all the better for being lonely, twelve inches away from its nearest neighbour. It will branch and bulge sideways, if you give it plenty of room to develop, and by August or September will have developed a middle-aged spread more desirable in plants than in human beings.

Some people do not like zinnias: they think them stiff and artificial-looking. But they are surely no more artificial-looking than dahlias, which they somewhat resemble, and their colours are even more subtle than the colours of the dahlia. In zinnias, you get a mixture of colours seldom seen in any other flower: straw-colour, greenish-white, a particular saffron-yellow, a dusky rose-pink, a coral-pink. The only nasty colour produced by the zinnia is a magenta; and this, alas, is produced only too often. When magenta threatens, I pull it up and throw it on the compost heap, and allow the lovelier colours to have their way. To conclude. Have you grown moluccella? It was introduced into this country from Syria in 1570, nearly 400 years ago, and seems to have been somewhat neglected until a recent revival of its popularity. I tried it and was disappointed when it first came up; then, as it developed, I saw that it did deserve its other name, the shell flower, and from being disappointed I came round to an affection for it. One must be patient with it, for it takes some leisurely summer weeks before it shows what it intends to do.

I was given to understand that it could be picked and kept in a vase indoors throughout the winter, but alas the ruthless hoe came along before I had time to arrest it, and my shell flower got carted off on to the rubbish heap.

*T*HOUGHTS FROM CHILE

I write these words in a Chilean garden, surrounded by a blaze of familiar flowers, petunias, zinnias, stocks, pansies, roses, all blooming with a generosity and an intensity of colour unknown to us at home. It is the height of summer. Outside in the streets are booths and barrows piled with every imaginable fruit, peaches, plums, apricots, nectarines, melons, grapes, all very luscious, but not what I had hoped to learn about the flora of Chile.

The one question everybody asked me was whether I knew their national flower called copihue. Reluctantly I had to say no; could they perhaps show me a specimen? Ah, they said, it does not grow in this part, the climate is too hot; you must go farther south, to the cooler and rainier district of Patagonia. I then accidentally discovered that the copihue was no other than our old friend, *Lapageria rosea*.

In England we usually treat this lovely climber as a greenhouse plant, where it grows happily away with its pendent trumpets of pink or red, but I do recall having seen it thriving with no more protection than the shelter of a glassed-in porch. This seems to indicate that we may enjoy it without artificial heat, and indeed I gather that it can be pretty cold in Patagonia.

If anyone is thinking of undertaking a botanical expedition to Chile, the time to come is the spring (September-October) when the rain brings a burst of flower all over the barren hills; on inquiry I found that calceolarias, nasturtiums, lupins, alstroemerias, and an indeterminate kind of amaryllis grow wild; also the climbing solanums in variety, relations of the potato which is a native of this country.

How ignorant one is! I never knew that we owed the strawberry to Chile. On the other hand, by an ungrateful twist of reciprocity, Chile owes England the black-berry. Some homesick emigrant brought it with him, and it took so kindly to its new home that it is now the curse of Chilean agriculture. Impossible to eradicate, strangling everything, it also becomes tinder-dry and bursts into flames, devastating wide areas and destroying everything except its own roots. It just shows how careful one ought to be about thoughtless transportation.

FRONT GARDENS

An English village street, gay with flowers, can be as pretty a sight as anyone could wish to see; and moreover is not to be found elsewhere in just that way, thanks to our climate and to the Englishman's passion for gardening. Most of these small front gardens are already well furnished with beds, but it would be pleasant to feel that something more permanent was also being planted, to commemorate the festival year of 1951, as things were planted to commemorate the Coronation in 1937.

Such permanent planting inevitably means trees or shrubs, both of which unfortunately have a habit of growing until they begin to obscure the light from the windows. Then the occupant of the house quite understandably prunes the poor thing back into a sort of mop head, when all its beauty is lost. A mop on top of a stick is very different from the loose, natural development of the mature plant smothered in flower or blossom. An ingenious way of getting out of this difficulty is to train the branches along post-and-wire, like an espalier apple or pear in an old kitchen garden. The flowering trees, by which I here mean the prunus, the pyrus, the Japanese cherries, the almonds, and all the other members of those lovely families, lend themselves very obligingly to such treatment, and I am sure prefer it to being hacked about and thwarted from what they want to do, which is to give as generously as they can of their load.

Have I made myself clear? No, I don't think I have. I often long to draw a little explanatory diagram, but for one thing I can't draw, and for another thing the newspaper could not print it if I could and did. So, without the aid of a diagram, may I suggest that you might run a row of flowering trees from your front gate to your front door, training them horizontally so that they will not obscure the light from your windows, and yet will make a path of blossom from gate to door along our village streets.

May I add a hint about rose hedges to grow along the pavement of a village street? Not necessarily a village, but a small country town, or even a suburb or a new housing estate; anywhere that seems to demand a hedge to divide the front garden from the road.

In a gracious, small and ancient town near where I live, someone has had the imagination to plant just such a hedge of rambler roses. It occupies the whole of his road frontage, about 150 yards I believe, and in the summer months people come from all over the county to see it. I must admit that it is an impressive sight; a blaze of colour; a long, angry, startling streak, as though somebody had taken a red pencil and had scrawled dense red bunches all over a thicket-fence of green. A splendid idea; very effective; but, oh, how crude! I blink on seeing it; and having blinked, I weep. It is not only the virulence of the colour that brings tears to my eyes, but the regret that so fine an idea should not have been more fastidiously carried out.

The hedge is made of 'American Pillar', a rose which, together with 'Dorothy Perkins', should be forever abolished from our gardens. I know this attack on two popular roses will infuriate many people; but if one writes gardening articles one must have the courage of one's opinion. I hate, hate, hate 'American Pillar' and her sweetly pink companion 'Perkins'. What would I have planted instead? Well, there is 'Goldfinch', an old rambler, very vigorous, very sweet-scented, and when I say sweet-scented I mean it, for I do try to tell the exact truth in these

Rosa 'Goldfinch'

articles, not to mislead anybody. 'Goldfinch' is a darling; she is my pet, my treasure; a mass of scrambled eggs. Then there is 'Félicité et Perpetué', white, flushed pink; and 'Madame Plantier', white, with larger flowers. Or 'Albertine', very strong and free-flowering, a beautiful soft pink that appears to have been dipped in tea; or 'François Juranville', which also appears to have fallen into a tea-cup.

It is not too late to plant now. You can plant anything between now and March.

MARCH

Sometimes in apple country you may see
A ghostly orchard standing all in white,
Aisles of white trees, white branches, in the green,
On some still day when the year hangs between
Winter and spring, and heaven is full of light.
And rising from the ground pale clouds of smoke
Float through the trees and hang upon the air,
Trailing their wisps of blue like a swelled cloak
From the round cheeks of breezes.

The Land

A MAD MARCH DREAM

It is agreeable sometimes to turn for a change from the dutifully practical aspects of gardening to the consideration of something strange, whether we can hope to grow it for ourselves or not. A wet March evening seemed just the time for such an indulgence of dreams, and in an instant I found my room (which hitherto had boasted only a few modest bulbs in bowls) filling up with flowers of the queerest colours, shapes, and habits. The first batch to appear, thus miraculously conjured out of the air, were all of that peculiar blue-green which one observes in verdigris on an old copper, in a peacock's feather, on the back of a beetle, or in the sea where the shallows meet the deep.

First came a slender South African, *Ixia viridiflora* with green flowers shot with cobalt blue and a purple splotch: this I had once grown in a very gritty pan in a cold greenhouse, and was pleased to see again. Then came the tiny sea-green Persian iris, only three inches high which I had seen lavishly piercing its native desert but had never persuaded into producing a single flower here. Then came *Delphinium macrocentrum*, an East African, which I had never seen at all.

There were quite a lot of birds in my room by now, as well as flowers, for *Strelitzia reginae* had arrived, escorted by the little African sun-birds which perch and powder their breast-feathers with its pollen. It is rare for plants to choose birds as pollinators instead of insects; and here was the best of them. *Strelitzia reginae* itself looked like a bird, a wild, crested, pointed bird, floating on an orange boat under spiky sails of blue and orange. Although it had been called *reginae* after Queen Charlotte, the consort of George III, I prefer its other name, the Bird of Paradise flower.

A mass of daffodils and blossom in the orchard.

Then as a change to homeliness, came clumps of the old primroses I had tried so hard to grow in careful mixtures of leaf-mould and loam, but here they were, flourishing happily between the cracks of the floorboards; 'Jack-in-the-Green', 'Prince Silverwings', 'Galligaskins', 'Tortoiseshell', 'Cloth of Gold'; and as I saw them there in a wealth I had never been able to achieve, I remembered that the whole *primula* family was gregarious in its tastes and hated the loneliness of being one solitary, expensive little plant. They like huddling together, unlike the lichens, which demand so little company that they will grow (in South America at any rate) strung out along the high isolation of telegraph wires. There seemed indeed no end to the peculiarities of plants, whether they provided special perches for the convenience of their visitors, or turned carnivorous like the pitcher plants. Why was it that the vine grew from left to right in the Northern Hemisphere, but refused to grow otherwise than from right to left in the Southern? Why was the poppy called *macounii* found only on one tiny arctic island in the Behring Sea and nowhere else in the world? How had it come there in the first place? In a room now overcrowded with blooms of the imagination such speculations flowed easily, to the exclusion of similar speculations on the equally curious behaviour of men.

The walls of the room melted away, giving place to a garden such as the Emperors of China once enjoyed, vast in extent, varied in landscape, a garden in which everything throve and the treasures of the earth were collected in beauty and brotherhood. But a log fell in the fire; a voice said: "This is the B.B.C. Home Service; here is the news", and I awoke.

Strelitzia reginae

SAVING BULBS FROM INDOORS

The time has come to plant out bulbs which have flowered in bowls in the house. If this is done regularly every year, it is surprising to see what a collection accumulates in a very short space of time, and how quickly they settle down to their new conditions. It may be true that a strongly forced bulb will not flower again, out of doors, until the second season, but as most of us start our bowls in a cool, dark cupboard and bring them into nothing more intense than the warmth of an ordinary living-room, which, in this country, is not saying much, the majority will reappear complete with bud twelve months hence.

It is no good whatsoever trying to preserve the early Roman hyacinths or the 'Paper White' narcissus, but all other hyacinths and all other narcissi (daffodils) lend themselves very obligingly to our wishes. Hyacinths should be planted shallow, with the nose of the bulb only just below soil-level. Narcissus wants to go deeper; and if you are planting in grass, as is the common practice, it is easy to cut three sides of a square of turf, hinge it back, set your bulbs in the hole, hinge the turf into place again, and stamp upon it with all the weight of Miss Jekyll's boots.

I treat my bowl-grown bulbs pretty rough. They must take their chance, as I must take mine. They have done their best for me, once, and if they will repeat even a second-best effort I shall be grateful. The most I do for them is to cut off their spent flowers to save them the effort of seeding, and make them a present of their green leaves necessary to the development of the bulb underground. These leaves look untidy for a bit, I know; they flop in a miserable dejective yellowing sheaf; the only thing to do with them if you want to keep them neat is to tie them into a knot of themselves. On no account cut them off.

You probably know all this already, so may I add two little reminders? It is so easy to forget these seasonal jobs, and then the moment has passed and it is too late. The first is to remember that March is the time to lift snowdrops, if you want to concentrate them instead of letting them remain scattered in odd clumps. Snow-drops do not mind being dug up while their leaf is still green; in fact, for some reason which I do not attempt to explain, it is the only way they enjoy removal. My second reminder applied to that brave little crocus, *tomasinianus*, which comes up in a mauve mist in February, and is now setting its seed.

It is interesting and very encouraging to see how crocuses can increase themselves over the years. If you want confirmation, go to Lacock Abbey, in Wiltshire, next March, where I should think at least an acre of short grass is spread like a purple rug in front of the grey old abbey beyond. It looked as though it had been laid down on purpose, yet nobody could conceivably have planted all those hundreds of thousands of corms, one by one, even in the days when one might have bought them for a penny a dozen and employed a boy at five shillings a week to plant them.

No. That great rug had spread itself by its own volition. It may have taken fifty years or more, but there was the result for us all to see, and to profit by the example.

Another hint I might give you. Pick off the crocuses' fading flowers now, and throw them down in wide patches over grass, say in a wild corner of the garden. The chances are that they will drop their seed, and reward you in three years' time.

*B*ROADCASTING SEEDS

The time for sowing seeds of hardy annuals is approaching. They can all be sown out of doors towards the middle or end of this half-way March month when an occasional spring-like day deludes us into a belief that winter is over – poor optimistic us! The birds share our optimism. They sing happily and madly because St Valentine is long past, as far back as February 14, their mating day when:

> *Smale fowles maken melodye*
> *That slepen al the night with open eye;*
> *So pricketh them Nature with hir corages.*

Nature must prick us with her courages also; and I would like to suggest that we might all go a bit bold and enterprising and altruistic this year, strewing our seeds all over the place, not only in our own prepared flower-beds, but also over such waste places as railway embankments, ruined castles, bomb-sites, and even along the hedgerows of our country lanes. Our wild flowers are dying out. They get ploughed up, or get cut down, in the interests of an urgent agricultural drive. We cannot hope to rescue the bulbous plants, such as our native orchises and Lent lilies, but we can at least repair some damage by scattering seed on the waste places. We have only to consider the way in which the rose bay willowherb has appeared all over London and other bombed cities; we have only to look at the way in which Canterbury bells and valerian spread over cliffs and embankments, far more lavishly than we would welcome in our small, cultivated, restricted gardens.

Years ago, I read a book by Maurice Hewlett. It was called *Rest Harrow*. It was about a man who went walking all over the country, sowing seeds broadcast. I have forgotten the detail of it, but I know it made a deep impresssion on me at the time, and I determined that if ever I got the chance I would go walking around, scattering seeds in handfuls, which might, or might not, come up. It was a youthful dream; but now that I am much, much older, and much more sadly experienced, I still believe that we might beautify our countryside by such rash sowings.

Seeds can be bought by the ounce or the pound, in mixtures, from most of the big seedsmen.

A PERSIAN MIMOSA

Many years ago, in the high mountains of Persia, I collected some seed pods off a mimosa which was most unaccountably growing there, some 5,000 feet above sea-level, and some hundred miles from any spot whence it could possibly be considered as a garden escape. I do not pretend to explain how it came there, in that cold, stony, snowy, desolate region; all I know is that there it was, and that I brought seeds home, and now have a tree of it growing out of doors in my garden and a vase full of it on my table, smelling not of the snows but of the warm South.

I think it is probably *Acacia dealbata* or *A. decurrens*, and not a true mimosa at all, but it looks so like what we call mimosa in the florists' shops or on the French Riviera that the name may conveniently serve. Botanists may write to tell me that it is more likely to be *Albizia julibrissin*, a native of Persia, whereas the acacia is a native of

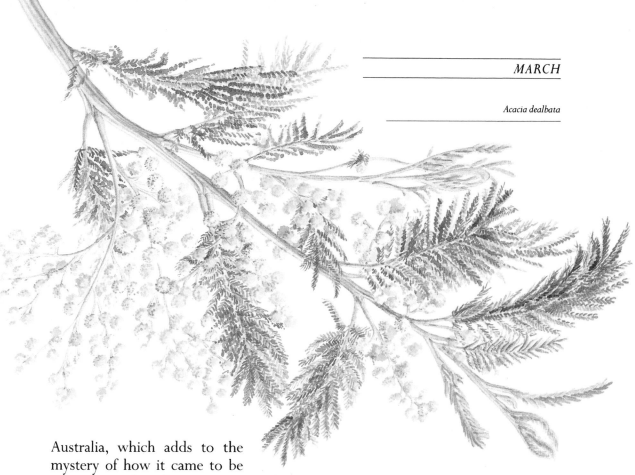

Acacia dealbata

Australia, which adds to the
mystery of how it came to be
growing on the Elburz mountains; but *Albizia* it certainly is not.

All this preamble is intended to suggest that enterprising gardeners in the south of England might well risk a plant in a sheltered corner. Of course the ideal place is a large conservatory, but few people nowadays have large conservatories. It might not come unscathed through a terrible winter such as we had in 1947, but my tree at any rate has not so far turned a hair in frost, and the place where I found it growing was certainly more bleak and windswept than anything we are likely to experience here. We take the precaution of wrapping its trunk and lower branches in trousers of sacking, and that is all the protection it gets. For greater safety, it could be trained fan-wise against a wall, if you started the training young enough. I should perhaps add that a high wall shelters it from the north, and that it is planted facing full south. It is no good picking it before the flowers are fully out, in the hope that they will open in water; there are some things which refuse to oblige in that way, and this is one of them. You must wait till the clusters are as fluffy and yellow as ducklings.

It makes a charming pot plant until it becomes too large and has to be transferred into a tub or else planted out into the open ground.

TWO TIPS FOR INDOORS

A friend and fellow traveller, herself an expert gardener, gave me a hint about the treatment of gladioli in water which she has been able successfully to demonstrate with the sheaves of the sword flower so fortunately at our disposal. You know that irritating habit the gladiolus has, of coming out at the bottom before it starts to come out at the top? My friend's system is simply to nip off the topmost bud or two,

Cornus mas

when all the lower ones hasten to open simultaneously. Apart from the obvious advantage of getting the whole lot fully expanded instead of being left with faded flowers low down while the higher ones are still sheathed in green, it greatly improves the appearance of the stalk, making it stand more erect and correcting its inclination to sag sideways as though it were thoroughly depressed and tired of life.

I wonder whether a similar decapitation would work in the open border?

Another gift for flower arrangers is that early March flowerer, the cornelian cherry, *Cornus mas*. A native of Europe, this small tree was long ago imported into this country and is probably so familiar that you will wonder why I mention it at all. It is because I have once again been astonished by its lasting properties when cut for the house; I honestly believe it would remain fresh for a month to six weeks, especially if cut before fully out and allowed to open its clusters of greenish-yellow gradually in the warmth of a room.

This virtue will appeal chiefly to the housewife concerned with getting "something to put in the vases that doesn't need renewing every few days", but the little tree should also appeal to the outdoor gardener who wants a resistant tough able to stand up to wind and frost, and decorative enough to make a soberly golden show against a pale blue sky.

ON THE EQUATOR

May I be forgiven if for once I make no attempt to be of any practical use in your garden at all? I am on the Equator as I write these notes, half way across the world, and, not being a blasé traveller, am far too preoccupied with the odd things I have seen and odd facts I have learnt to think soberly of the duties which confront the gardener in an English spring.

Amongst the odd though perhaps not very useful bits of information I have picked up, I never knew that coffee, like the pigeon orchid, flowered after a sudden drop in temperature, in the case of the orchid exactly and invariably nine days; I did not know that more tapioca was used in the manufacture of glue and glossy paper for illustrated magazines than for all the milk puddings in the world's nurseries, nor that kapok came from a forest tree with a hollow trunk that echoes like a drum, nor that the frangipani tree was planted in cemeteries for the scented blooms, in falling, to carpet the graves, nor that monkeys could be trained to collect rare orchids from the

tops of trees, nor that the Malayans used coral instead of stone in their rock-gardens. I had never realised that annuals, given tropical conditions, would produce seeds within three months of sowing and, since they flower continuously in countries where winter is unknown, would supply four generations in one year. Nor had I ever been sufficiently grateful for not living in an island where the local burglar blows the pollen of datura in through your open window by means of a blowpipe, and helps himself to your possessions while you lie temporarily insensible.

Of the beauty of some flowering trees it would be tantalising to speak, for many of them cannot be induced to flower for us, even given the appropriate warmth and humidity of a greenhouse. This, apparently, is due to the extreme importance of long hours of daylight. Whether the difficulty could be overcome by artificial rays remains to be seen. There are reports that it is being tried in America.

WORTHWHILE LOBELIA

I wish to emphasise the virtues of lobelia, properly employed. This sadly mis-used annual has suffered more than most from the Victorian system of bedding-out. It seems condemned forever to an association with white alyssum, in a ribbon-development along the front of a bed or border. Dot blue, dot white, dot blue, dot white . . . dot blue; and, into the bargain, it is usually the nastiest form of lobelia, dark navy-blue, the colour of a school-girl's gym suit, with a malicious little peeping white eye, the school-girl spying on her school-fellows, a horribly ugly little plant, not to be compared with the bright lobelia called 'Cambridge Blue'.

This is a really worthwhile annual, a pure clear blue; a gentian blue. One should use it in many unconventional ways, jolting and bumping it out of the bad habits it has been taught to regard as proper to its existence.

For example, I have got an old copper discarded from an old laundry in favour of something more up to date, a vast thing I found thrown away in a bed of nettles; of little value in terms of shillings and pence, but of the utmost value to me now that it has turned that peculiar viridian or apple-green which suggests a Ptolemaic antiquity. This object I propose to cram with a tight thick huge bun of 'Cambridge Blue' for this summer, so dense that you could run your hand over it and ruffle it as though it were fur. It may be a success; it may not. If it is a failure, I shall not repeat the experiment.

SPARE THE ROSES

We now approach the time of year when thoughts turn towards the pruning of roses. Knives and secateurs are now at their sharpest. Brandishing these objects of destruction, battalions of professional and amateur gardeners advance, prepared to do their worst, as they have immemorially been taught. The word of command has gone out: "Cut almost to the ground; cut down to the second or third bud; cut till nothing is left except a couple of inches sticking up. Be pitiless, be ruthless; prune for fine blooms, exhibition blooms, even if you don't intend to exhibit. Never mind about the appearances of your garden, or the natural alacrity of your roses. Snub them as hard as you can, even as Victorian parents snubbed their children".

It rejoices me to see that different ideas are creeping in. The rose, even the hybrid teas and the hybrid perpetuals, is no longer to be regarded as a stunted dwarf, but as a wildly blossoming shrub. Let her grow up, even to three or four feet in height, and throw her head about as I believe she was meant to.

This truth first dawned upon me during the war, when as a Land Army representative I had occasion to visit many small gardens in pursuit of owners who had been called away. Their gardens were turning into a sad disorder of weeds, but the roses reared themselves up, superb and proud, just because they had not been interfered with for two, three, four, five years. Then in the well-kept garden of a friend I saw similar rose bushes which, she assured me, had scarcely been touched since she planted them thirty years ago. She had merely snipped the tips; had taken out the dead wood and the weak growth; and for the rest had left them to their will. The result was lavish and surprising.

My liking for gardens to be lavish is an inherent part of my garden philosophy. I like generosity wherever I find it, whether in gardens or elsewhere. I hate to see things scrimp and scrubby. Even the smallest garden can be prodigal within its own limitations, and I would now suggest that you should try the experiment of not slaughtering your roses down to almost ground level, at least for this year; and see what happens.

AN EXTRAORDINARY SURVIVOR

I have just planted out a *Metasequoia glyptostroboides*. In case this name should by any chance sound unfamiliar, I should explain that it refers to a tree whose discovery was one of the romances of plant-collecting. It had been known for some time as a fossil going back to the Mesozoic era, which I understand occurred some 200,000,000 years ago, but as no living specimen had ever been seen, botanists assumed that it had gone out of existence at about the same time as its contemporaries the giant reptiles. The surprise of a Mr T. Wang can therefore be imagined, when, in the year 1946, he observed three strange conifers growing in a remote valley of North-Eastern Szechuan. Their foliage corresponded to the fossil remains. Further exploration revealed the somewhat patchy presence of other similar trees in the same area, growing for the most part beside streams in marshy places; seed was collected, and, since it germinates readily, this extraordinary survivor from a fantastically distant age may now be regarded as safe for future generations in Europe and America.

It seems unlikely that many owners of small gardens will feel inspired to plant one, for its eventual height of 130 ft. may prove as intimidating as its name. Nevertheless, as young specimens can already be seen growing in some private and some public gardens, such as Kew and Wisley, I might as well describe their appearance so that you can recognise a *Metasequoia* when you meet one. Pale green and feathery in spring and summer, it turns bright pink in autumn, a really startling sight when the sunshine catches it. Judging by my own experience from a tiny seedling given to me, it grows very fast, about six feet in as many years, especially if planted in the damp situation it loves.

I did not plant mine in a damp situation; I kept it in a pot, not knowing what to do with it; and it grew and grew, becoming more and more pot-bound, poor thing, but still thriving. It throve so well under these unkind conditions that I have now felt bound to reward it by letting it out into a damp gully in the middle of a field, where, if no cow eats it, I shall watch its progress with considerable interest.

KAFFIR LILIES

I don't believe I have ever mentioned *Schizostylis coccinea*, more palatably known as the Kaffir lily. It is a thing to grow at the foot of a south wall, in well-drained soil which nevertheless will not dry out too stringently in summer, or the tuberous roots will not build themselves up to the plumpness necessary for the next crop of flowers. This condition does sound rather contradictory, I know; but do not let it deter you from investing in a handful of Kaffir lilies to plant this month of March. This is the time to do it. Set them about three inches deep.

The Kaffir lily, which resembles a small gladiolus, produces its red or rosy spikes of flower in the late autumn, October, and even into November, which I call winter. In mild climates such as Cornwall, the Scillies and the Channel Islands I am assured that it goes on flowering right into March. Lucky people to enjoy so obliging a temperature. A correspondent from Alderney tells me that his Kaffir lilies do best in semi-shade; I can make no comment on this statement, but pass it on for the consideration of other growers; I should have thought, myself, that a South African needed all the sun baking it could get.

In the ordinary state of the thermometer in the rest of our dear island, it does need a touch of love and cherishment – another way of saying that it is not as hardy as we might wish. It would like a scatter of protective bracken over its roots in frosty weather. If you can give it this, it will reward you by coming up year after year, but if you can't be bothered to protect it out of doors you can grow it as a pot-plant in an unheated greenhouse or on the window-sill of a living room. It lends itself very kindly to pot treatment, but of course anybody who grows it like this in a pot will realise that it won't go on indefinitely in the same pot without being tipped out and re-potted into fresh soil every spring.

Schizostylis coccinea 'Mrs Hegarty'

There is only one species of the Kaffir lily. There are variants, called 'Mrs Hegarty' and 'Viscountess Byng'. I think 'Mrs Hegarty' is the most recommendable, so pretty in her pink frock, but some people say that 'Lady Byng' is the better do-er. Try these two ladies out for yourselves. Personally I shall stick to 'Mrs Hegarty' because I know her and have never yet been introduced to 'Lady Byng', which is no reason why one should not make a new friend of 'Lady Byng' What is life, and what is gardening, if one is not always ready to make new friends and make new experiments?

DARLING DAISIES

Some people like daisies in their turf; others don't. Jean-Jacques Rousseau ascribed pinky eyelashes to it, thought it a general favourite, and called it the *robin* of flowers. To John Skelton it was "daisie delectable". Beaumont and Fletcher thought it "smell-less, yet most quaint", incorrectly, for a bunch of daisies has a peculiarly earthy smell, especially when it comes as a hot little gift in the hand of a child. Wordsworth, peering closely, noticed that it cast a shadow to "protect the lingering dewdrop from the sun". Tennyson, who was usually extremely accurate about such matters, went very wrong when he claimed for Maud that

> . . . her feet have touched the meadows
> And left the daisies rosy,

for this is simply not true. Enchanted by this idea, I wasted many youthful summer hours stamping on daisies, in fact I still do, but never a daisy has so far blushed beneath my tread.

Fortunately for those who like their turf green and not speckled, it is very easy for them to reverse the old song and give their answer to Daisy. A selective weed-killer will do the trick economically and with a great saving of labour, though it may be necessary to go twice with the lethal watering-can over the ground. Good turf certainly looks better just after it has been mown, without those flattened patches, though there is perhaps something to be said for the small "companion of the sun" when it has reappeared within a day or two.

Bellis perennis 'Dresden China'

The cultivated varieties of *Bellis perennis* come under quite a different heading. These will be grown in soil, not in grass, and are most evocative of old kitchen gardens where they were so often used as edging to paths. The cottagey 'Hen-and-Chickens' should never be forgotten: it consorts well with the double primroses, for anyone who can persuade these charming but fickle creatures to thrive. 'Rob Roy', a deep red, is somewhat smaller and less domestically minded; 'Alice', with a Victorian suggestion in her name, is suitably pink and quilled. A tiny variety, best suited to a trough or the rock-garden, is the bright pink 'Dresden China', truly as pretty as porcelain, the perfect companion both in scale and character to our native forget-me-not, *Myosotis alpestris*. These daisies are all hardy, but are best renovated from time to time by pulling the clumps to pieces and replanting firmly. I wonder whether the old gardeners ever troubled to do this? Plants seem to exact far more attention nowadays. They seem to be aware that they live in a Welfare State and to resent being left to take care of themselves.

NOSTALGIC AURICULAS

Nostalgia for the past has brought with it a revival of taste for the old-fashioned flowers: the flaked pinks and carnations, the double primroses, the old roses, the broken tulips, the double sweet william. Perhaps it is not only nostalgia for an age which, rightly or wrongly, we esteem to have been happier than our own, as it was certainly more leisurely, but also a natural reaction against the exaggerated blooms we are offered to-day: size not subtlety. Who wants a begonia like a saucer?

Amongst the many plants thus returning to favour, the auricula finds its little place. I am not here concerned with the outdoor, or alpine, auricula, so familiar in cottage gardens, but with what is known as the Show auricula, which must be grown indoors or under glass, not because it fails in hardiness but because the powder (farina) gets washed off in the rain and all its essentially cleanly character is lost. It cannot afford to get itself into a mess. Neatest and most exquisitely demarcated of flowers, it must keep itself as trim as the fireside cat. Given this opportunity, it will produce in April and May flower-heads which combine at one and the same time a demure simplicity and an appearance of extreme sophistication. Grey; green; white edged with green; scarlet edged with green; yellow edged with grey; the variations are manifold. The old growers used to put their pots on ranged shelves, sometimes fitted into a small home-made theatre with scenery painted behind it as a background.

To be practical about raising the auriculas. They are expensive to buy as plants, but cheap to grow from a packet of seed from the best firm. Sow in April in a pan of very finely sifted soil, and scarcely cover the seed. This is important; if too deeply buried the seed will refuse to germinate. Prick the seedlings out into tiny pots, and pot up singly into four-inch pots, never into a big pot. Keep them cool always, never exposed to a hot sun.

APRIL

But for this summer's quick delight
Sow marigold, and sow the bright
Frail poppy that with noonday dies
But wakens to a fresh surprise;
Along the pathway stones be set
Sweet alysson and mignonette,
That when the full midsummer's come
On scented clumps the bees may hum,
Golden Italians, and the wild
Black humble-bee alike beguiled:
And lovers who have never kissed
May sow the cloudy love-in-mist.

The Land

LONG-LOST ROSES

This, I fear, is not going to be very practical. It will be of no use at all to anybody who is making or planting a garden. But as it will appear on All Fools' Day I may perhaps be allowed a frivolity for once.

The frivolity concerns a nurseryman's catalogue dated 1838. Queen Victoria had recently come to the throne. One of her humbler subjects, Mr John Miller, of the Durdham Down Nursery, near Bristol, had just died as a bankrupt. His executors were carrying on his business, for the benefit of the creditors including the bankrupt's immediate relatives.

Poor Mr John Miller. He had a magnificent list of plants for disposal, not only roses, but geraniums, auriculas, pinks, orchids, herbaceous plants – pages and pages of them. It seems a shame that he should go smash so soon after his young Queen had embarked on a reign of over sixty years of prosperity.

The reason why I here revive his list is not so much because I feel sorry for Mr Miller, dead and lost 113 years ago, as because I think his catalogue may interest rose specialists and may also appeal to those who share my appreciation for such names as these, picked at random: 'Monstrous Four Seasons'; 'Assemblage des Beautés'; 'Belle Sans Flatterie'; 'Black African'; 'La Belle Junon'; 'Ninon de l'Enclos'; 'Temple d'Apollon'; 'Conque de Venus'.

Where have they gone, these bearers of fantastically romantic names? If Edmond Rostand had known of them he would surely have put a great speech about them into the mouth of Cyrano de Bergerac. Where are they now? Lost, I suppose, for ever, unless they could be discovered in some ancient garden in England or France.

Pleached limes and spring flowers in the Lime Walk.

One of those queer quirks of memory that sometimes assail us made me take down from my shelves a copy of *The Rose Fancier's Manual*, by Mrs Gore, once a best-seller amongst novelists. I found, as I expected, that Mrs Gore's book exactly corresponded in date, 1838, with the list of Mr Miller, deceased. She mentions a number of the same roses, but she also mentions others which Mr Miller had not got, or perhaps had sold out of. Her 'Coupe d'Amour' does not figure in Mr Miller's list; nor does 'Tout Aimable'; nor does the rose whose name, if truthful, makes me want to possess it more than any: 'Rien Ne Me Surpasse'. Surely the most exacting should be satisfied with that.

THE CHARM OF CORONILLA

Easter Day. It seems odd to look back to Christmas Day, but there is a gay little butter-yellow shrub in my garden which has been flowering continuously between those two great feasts of the Church, a sort of hyphen linking the Birth and the Resurrection, which is more than can be said for most shrubs, so I think it deserves a write-up, as these recommendations are colloquially called, and a tribute of gratitude for the pleasure it has given me in its persistence throughout the dreary months. The shrub I mean is called *Coronilla glauca*.

There are several sorts of coronilla. I know I shall be told that *Coronilla emerus* is the hardier, but on the whole I should advise *glauca*. I know I shall be told that it isn't quite hardy. I know it isn't supposed to be, but all I can say is that it came through the frightening frosts of February 1956, with no protection, and if a supposedly tender shrub can survive that test, it qualifies for at least a trial in the Home Counties and the south-west, though perhaps not in the Midlands, East Anglia, or the north. I must admit also that I planted it in a narrow border under the south-facing wall of the house, where it got the maximum of shelter against cold north winds or east winds; and there it still is, flowering exuberantly away, one of the most delightful surprises and successes I ever had.

I must add another word in praise of this rarely planted shrub. It has its own sense of humour. Sometimes it gives off so strong a scent as to delude me into thinking that I

Coronilla glauca

caught the scent of some neighbouring wallflowers; then I discovered that the coronilla is powerfully fragrant by day and scentless by night.

This whole question of scent in plants is one which I do not understand, though no doubt a scientific explanation is available. The warmth of the sun and the humidity of rain and dew account for much, as we all know from observation and experience, but there must be other factors unrevealed to the ignoramus. Why, for instance, does the balsam poplar waft its scent a hundred yards distant sometimes and at other times remain so obstinately scentless and sniffless as to be imperceptible on the closest approach? These things retain their mystery for me, and I am not sure that I want the answer.

May I assure the gentleman who writes to me (quite often) from a priory in Sussex that I am not the armchair, library fireside gardener he evidently suspects, "never having performed any single act of gardening" myself, and that for the last forty years of my life I have broken my back, my finger-nails, and sometimes my heart, in the practical pursuit of my favourite occupation?

*T*HE EASTER MAGNOLIA

The great white *Magnolia denudata*, or Yulan tree, began to open its flowers along its leafless branches on Easter Saturday, a magnificent sight against the pale blue of the April sky. The cool weather we endured throughout February and March suited its arrangements perfectly, for a warm spell during the early months tends to hurry it up, and then the flowers are liable to damage by their two enemies, frost and wind. I wonder that this most lovely of flowering trees is not more often planted. It is of reasonably rapid growth, eventually attaining a height of between twenty and forty feet, and, unlike some of the other magnolias such as *kobus* and *campbellii*, has the merit of flowering when still quite young. Any good garden loam suits it, especially if some decayed leaf mould can be added. It is best planted in April or May, so there is still time this year, and the vital thing to remember is that it must never be allowed to suffer from drought before it has become established. Once firmly settled into its new home, it can be left to look after itself. Avoid planting it in a frost pocket, or in a position where it will be exposed to the rays of a warm sun after a frosty night: under the lee of a north or west wall is probably the ideal situation, or within the shelter of a shrubbery.

This dignified and comely tree has been known in our gardens since 1789, when it was introduced from China by one of the collectors financed by that enlightened patron of plant-hunters, Sir Joseph Banks. In China it had been known for far longer than that; in fact, for some 1300 years, growing beside temples and in the garden of the Summer Palace. Presumably it gets caught by frost in its native home also; frost spells ruin to the year's crop of flowers, and people who for reasons of limited space feel unwilling to take the risk in spite of the immense reward in a favourable season, would be better advised to plant the later-flowering *Magnolia soulangiana*, less pure in its whiteness, for the outside of the petals is stained with pink or purple; or *Magnolia soulangiana* 'Lennei', which is frankly rosy, but very beautiful with its huge pink goblets, and seldom suffers from frost unless it has extremely bad luck at the end of

Azara microphylla

April or when those three mischievous ice-saints hold their festival in the middle of May.

A VANILLA SCENTED SHRUB

A very pleasing little shrub or small tree, not often seen in gardens, has been in flower since the middle of March. It is not at all showy, and most people would pass it by without noticing, unless they happened to catch a whiff of the scent. It is pure vanilla. This is *Azara microphylla*.

I would hesitate to recommend it except to gardeners who want something their neighbour probably hasn't got; but, after all, it is for those gardeners that I write. Gardeners who want something different from the usual, and yet something easy to grow. *Azara microphylla* is quite easy to grow. It is an evergreen; it has neat little shiny leaves that look as though they had been varnished; and it has this tiny yellow flower which is now spreading its scent over my writing table and into the whole of my room. I sit and sniff. Wafts of vanilla come to me as I write.

Azara microphylla is a native of Chile, in South America. Some authorities say that it is not hardy here in Britain except in the favoured climate of Devon or Cornwall. I don't believe this. I have got it thriving where I live in Kent, and I have seen a twenty-foot-high tree of it in the rather colder climate of Gloucestershire. So I would say: plant it and risk it.

It likes to be planted in leaf mould. It would do well trained on to a wall with a north, or east, or west aspect; by which I mean that the early morning sun would not get at it after a frosty night. This is always an important point to remember when you are planting things affected by frost and by the warm morning sun which comes as too great a shock after the chill of the night. Plants must be let down gently. The transition must not be too quick.

UNDER GLASS

Looking back over the nastiest weeks of our late unlamented winter, I try to remember with gratitude the things that gave me pleasure when all was grey and colourless and cold outside. I managed then to keep a few square yards on a shelf or staging in an unheated greenhouse, and those few square yards were crowded with tiny bright things from New Year's Day to Easter. Their brilliance contrasted with the snow and the leaden skies; it was like coming into an aviary of tropical birds or butterflies, yet they were all easy to grow, nothing odd or recondite, just a few pans of the early species crocus; a pot of *Cyclamen coum* which flowered so madly I thought it might kill itself by its generosity; a pan-full of grape hyacinths dug up out of the garden; some snowdrops lifted just before they intended to flower; some saxifrages sprouting into miniature nail-head-size of flower, hugging close to the tight grey-green rosettes they pinkly star; some early flowering narcissi and jonquils; a pot-plant of the lovely pink *Camellia* 'Donation'; some early primulas, *frondosa* and *marginata* var. 'Linda Pope'; a pot of the scented *Daphnes collina* and *tangutica*; and, bravest and earliest of all, the miniature sky-blue *Iris histrioides* 'Major', which I recommend to everybody, either for indoors or out. It is ideal in an alpine pan and ideal in a sink or trough. A sprinkling of grey granite or limestone chippings goes a long way towards enhancing the colour and delicacy of the flowers.

The great advantage of keeping these small things under glass is that you get them unblemished by weather, which only too often tears the petals and splashes them with mud. Besides, one often gets delightful surprises. I got one. In the autumn I had been dividing some of the six-inch-high *Iris pumila*, and put some spare rhizomes into flat pans for growing on my shelf. Mysterious seedlings appeared, obviously not a weed; I left them and they developed into sturdy little plants of a viola which I take to be 'Huntercombe Purple'; the seeds must have been lying dormant in the soil. They flowered at the same time as the irises, making a pretty if unorthodox combination almost the same colour as the darker form of the *Iris atropurpurea*, and making an equally good foil to the pale blue of *Iris coerulea*. Such simple happenings give extravagant pleasure. I have a disquieting suspicion that deliberate attempts might not prove nearly so satisfactory. Nature sometimes has ideas of her own which are better than ours.

*H*APHAZARD JOTTINGS

So many ideas occur to one in this exciting season of the year that it is difficult to keep them tidy. So I must just jot them down haphazard, and number them one, two, three.

ONE. The delicious scents that reach us on the air. Tracking them down in my own garden in April, I find that they sometimes emanate from the Chinese shrub, *Osmanthus delavayi*, clothed with its clusters of white flower. (It would make an ideal and unusual hedge, being evergreen, and growing only to the convenient height of six or eight feet. Also it does not seem to mind how cruelly you chop it about.)

More frequently, since I have only one plant of osmanthus, not a whole hedge, it is the balsam poplar that leads my nose around, sniffing, and puzzles visitors to my garden as much as it puzzles me. I struggled and struggled to obtain the true balsam poplar; I kept on buying it from nurserymen under various names, but it never smelt as good as I knew it ought to smell. Finally, I tore some bits from a tree in a friend's old garden, and got the real thing. They strike so readily and grow so fast. You just stick them in, and they make roots.

TWO. Daffodils. Many people have complained that their daffodils did not flower this spring as well as usual. This puzzled me, because mine growing in grass in an old orchard seemed to flower as well as ever. I think the explanation must be that the narcissus family did not enjoy the warm baking they got during the summer of 1959, as other bulbs enjoyed it, and that my old orchard remained fairly damp, not to say water-logged, throughout the hot summer.

There is also the question of whether one should divide the clumps. Yes, I suppose one should, and replant them separately; but that is a long job if you have a lot of bulbs to cope with. What I do believe in is dead-heading, by which I mean cutting off the seedpods before they form, unnecessarily robbing the bulb of its sustenance.

THREE. Viburnums. What a valuable shrub this is for the time of year. *Viburnum burkwoodii* is in full flower, and so is *V. bitchiuense.* We ought to plant them more recklessly in odd out-of-the-way corners of our gardens, and let them grow up, and let them develop, and then suddenly notice what a success we have achieved.

A VINE HEDGE
I would like to pick up the ancient idea of making a hedge of vines. To do this, you allow your young vine to develop only one single rod, which you train horizontally, along a wire or along bamboo canes if you prefer, nailed to pegs driven into the soil; and when this rod has reached a length of thirteen feet, you bend the end of it downwards and push it firmly to a depth of six inches or more into the ground. It will then take root (we hope), and will spring up quite soon in new growth for the next rod, when you repeat the process, over and over again until your original vine with its recurrent progeny has attained the length you require.

You see the advantages. First, you need only one root-stock to start the process: very economical. (Of course, if you liked to plant two, one at either end, it would go quicker, and they would meet in the middle, like engineers working through an alpine tunnel.) Secondly, you can control your rods into any shape to suit the layout of your garden; you could grow them in a straight line down a long path, for example, or you could make them turn sharp corners at right angles to form an enclosure, vines being very flexible and tractable. Thirdly, by the time the rods have made old wood they should need no propping or staking; they will have grown tough enough to support themselves. Fourthly, you can, if you wish, grow this serialised vine a mile long. What a thought! Fifthly, you can eat the grapes.

B LOODROOT
It surprises me to find that in all these years I have never mentioned *Sanguinaria canadensis*, the bloodroot of Canada.

Arriving home from abroad about the middle of March, I found a thriving little colony of this exquisitely pretty thing in full flower. By a thriving little colony I mean that it had increased itself since I first planted it. That meant that it was doing well, and was happy where I had put it.

Plants are very fickle. Some hepaticas which I had planted at the same time near the sanguinaria in the correct belief that they would enjoy the same conditions of leaf mould and half shade, have simply failed to reappear this year. Yes, I know that hepaticas hate being transplanted and take two or three years to settle down, but mine had had time to settle down and I thought they were established for life. Not at all. They have vanished.

The sanguinaria on the other hand is thriving. It could not be described as a showy plant. It is not for people who want a great splash of colour. It is for people who like looking quietly into the delicacy and subtlety of blue-grey leaves, shell-pink buds, and stems whose tender pink seems to complement the opening flower.

It should be planted, I think, in a shady pocket of a rock garden, if you cannot give it the woodland conditions it likes. I can imagine it coming up through such woodland things as the erythroniums or dog's-tooth violets, or that other North American woodlander the Trinity flower, *Trillium erectum*, but who among us can indulge ourselves in such dreams as these? We must be content with our one little colony.

If you do decide to grow the sanguinaria in your garden, I would give you an extra word of advice. Mark its site very carefully with a large label, because it disappears underground during the summer and you won't know where it was. And if you want to increase your clump, you must propagate it by division in August, but unless you are a very skilled gardener, I would advise you to let it alone. I am all for letting things alone, without interference, if they seem happy where they are. The sanguinaria belongs to the poppy family, and generally speaking the poppies don't like being shifted about.

So much for the Canadian bloodroot, a plant for gardeners of fastidious taste. On the opposite side of the scale, I have received an advertisement from the *New York Times* which fills me with horror. It is headlined: "Plant thousands of flowers in sixty seconds, with instant planting, a carpet of flowers". Automatic gardening come true.

It seems that you can buy a pre-seeded Plant-a-mat that unrolls like a rug, and you lay it down as you would a stair-carpet, and within no time at all you have a fabulous garden with thousands of giant blooms, rainbow colours, and spectacular effects.

Well, well . . . I think I shall still prefer the Canadian bloodroot.

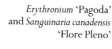

Erythronium 'Pagoda'
and *Sanguinaria canadensis*
'Flore Pleno'

GERBERAS IN POTS

G Unfortunately the gerbera, or Barberton daisy, from Natal and the Transvaal is not reliably hardy in this country unless in some very mild district it can be planted at the foot of a south wall. Otherwise it is best in a cool greenhouse, where as a pot plant it will flower through summer and into autumn. Given a very little heat, say a temperature of 50° F., it will flower pretty nearly all round the year.

It appears to engender an endless supply of its tall, daisy-like flowers in an amazing range of those shades so regrettably known as pastel. Coral, butter, straw, salmon, lavender, cream; and then some stronger colours in red and orange. I would suggest half a dozen plants in a very large pot or even in a wooden tub. April is the best time to obtain and start them. Good drainage and a fairly rich light soil mixed with some handfuls of peat and sand will suit them. They like plenty of moisture, so long as it does not stagnate and above all, does not gather in or round the crown, when it may cause the only serious trouble gerberas suffer from, namely a kind of foot rot, for which the only remedy is the bonfire. This should be easily preventable by a scatter of stone chippings on the surface.

Gerberas excel as a picked flower. They last for several weeks; I have kept them for close on a month, and very lovely they look in the evenings under a tall table-lamp.

I must add a postscript for the especial benefit of the enthusiastic amateur who enjoys making experiments. Hand pollination may produce variations of colour, in other words the colour range of the Barberton daisy has not yet been fully exploited, and anything might turn up. How exciting that would be! Supposing one produced a green or a blue gerbera, suddenly? Sensation at the R.H.S. fortnightly show.

Then there is another postscript I must add, of no interest except to expert growers, and perhaps not even to them. All the same, I think it should be recorded, as it seems to contradict everything we have been taught to say about good drainage, open soil and so forth.

Well, the finest gerberas I ever saw grown in a private garden in England were planted in a raised bed of turves turned upside down, sopping wet, in a cool house. If I had been given that bed to deal with, I should have planted ferns. Expert growers, explain this as you can.

OLD-FASHIONED WISDOM

*Some peoples can grow things
and some peoples can't.*

This remark was made to me many years ago by one of those old-fashioned gardeners of a type now nearly extinct, and although he probably did not know the correct name of any plant he grew in the herbaceous border under his charge he did know how to grow it and make it give its best.

◆

*Clematis alpina growing out of a large urn with Fritillaria imperialis in the
background.*

Huge they were, towering hollyhocks, vast delphiniums, lumps of galega, all arranged in heights, and how superbly grown, and how displeasing to our present-day taste.

I often wish I could recall that old gardener to life, and show him how different our gardens are today. Yet do I? He might be hurt and offended and horrified by the informal muddle we now make of our gardens. He would not understand why we no longer desire the great herbaceous borders, but prefer the more intimate and manageable confusion that we can look after for ourselves.

He would be shocked by the way we allow things he would have regarded as weeds to sow themselves all over the place. My own garden, for example, is overrun by wild violets, white and purple. I let them spread.

The yellow wallflower and the butter-and-eggs snapdragon sow themselves in my old brick walls; I let them increase. I know they are not very choice, but they look right where they have chosen to set themselves, and so I leave them. Forget-me-nots appear where I have never planted them, and give an unexpected patch of blue.

The blue *Anemones blanda* and *apennina* crop up in the grass of an orchard where no professional gardener would ever have dreamt of trying them. Rosemary, self-sown, flourishes in solid masonry; I could never have persuaded it to grow there if it had not elected to do so of its own accord. The pink *Clematis montana* 'Rubens' is a wildly prolific self-sower; it would smother walls if not kept in check.

The luckiest chance I ever had was a seedling of *Clematis armandii*, carried by some obliging bird and dropped into a discarded copper I had rescued from some old laundry. The copper had acquired that strange viridian green that copper does acquire with age, and looked like something excavated from an Egyptian tomb, B.C. I should never have had the imagination to train a white clematis around it, had the bird not invented it for me.

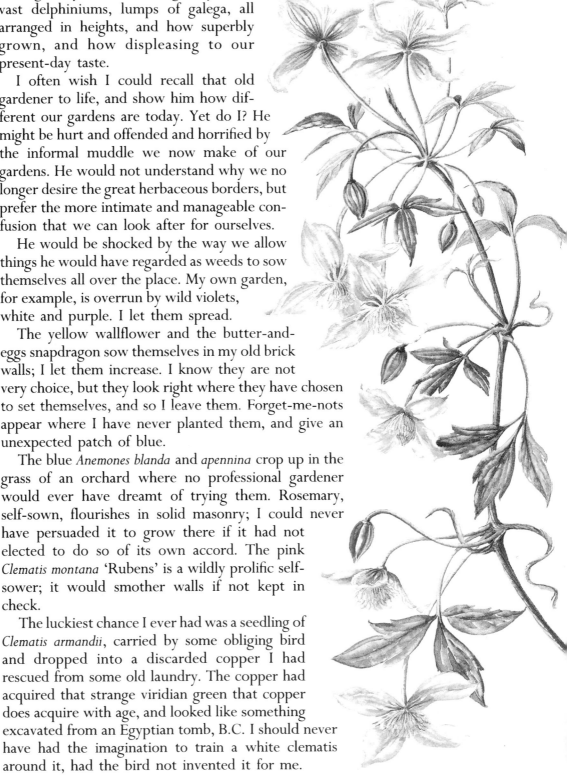

My old gardener, with his tidy mind, would turn in his grave. "Oh, Miss Vita", he would say, "how can you write such dreadful things? What, them nasty common weeds coming up here and there where they ain't wanted? No, that ain't my idea of gardening. Not one little bit it ain't."

DETERRING BIRDS
A very pretty, clean little tree which has been in flower since the middle of this month is the golden-barked Manchurian cherry, *Prunus maackii*. With its pale green leaves and masses of tiny white flowers, it makes a change from the innumerable pinks and reds of the flowering trees one now sees in most gardens. I called it a little tree, because mine is not very big, but I believe that eventually it will grow to a height of forty feet. It must then be a lovely sight.

My thanks to all those who have written about remedies against the attack of sparrows on primroses. For the benefit of other sufferers, of whom there appear to be many, I append a list of recommendations, which of course would apply equally to attacks on other flowers, such as the yellow crocus, a particular victim. Pepper seems to be the favourite deterrent, though rather an expensive one; but dry mustard, flowers of sulphur, Keatings powder, soot, powdered naphthalene, quassia, soft soap, paraffin-and-water, saffron, Jeyes fluid, Izal, and basic slag are all mentioned. Earthenware saucers sunk into the ground and filled with water find great favour. Wire pea-guards (to be removed daily after breakfast), wire netting to be bent into the shape of a mob-cap over each plant, fish-netting, the old nursery fireguard, old hairnets, sprigs of holly, and "an ordinary dark glass bottle on the ground", have all been found helpful. Some handfuls of confetti have also been found to do the trick.

Among things to dangle, I am advised to use Glitterbangs, tin foil, potatoes stuck with pheasants' feathers, pieces of bright blue paper, a bell, and the coloured tops of milk bottles. I am most grateful to the gentleman who sent me a regular necklace of these. Among the unkinder remedies I find mousetraps, bright unbreakable beads for the sparrows to break their beaks upon, "the body of a sparrow on a little gibbet", and "a masterful young cat". It seems, however, that an old fur among the plants will take the place of real cats, and that a pair of white china dogs has proved very efficacious. A palisade of wooden pipe lighters is advised, also of bits of looking glass or of old gramophone records, splintered, "preferably

Clematis montana 'Rubens' and *Rosmarinus officinalis*

Bing Crosby". One humanitarian advocates a sparrow corner where the offenders may disport themselves in sand boxes and bird baths, and may amuse themselves with the sweet william, sorrel, and spinach that you will have provided for them; but not all the sufferers are humanitarians, and in cases of great exasperation a shotgun or a catapult may be brought into action.

I have left to the last the question of cotton. Apparently I went wrong in using strong black thread. I ought to have used thin cotton, of the 50 variety, and not thread at all. Even blue cotton would have been better. I apologise. And now you can take your choice.

SMALL IRISES

There is a race of little irises, flowering in April and May, too seldom grown. They do not aspire to make a great splash; their colours are frail; they grow only six to twelve inches high; they demand a small place to match their small size; they must be regarded as intimate flowers, to be peered into and protected from the vulgar slug; I am referring to miniature versions of the Bearded Iris, which is the most familiar sort. These miniature versions are called *pumila* and *chamaeiris*.

I will not waste space quarrelling over botanical differences. I will say only that if you can buy what nurserymen usually call *Iris pumila* you will get a reward. Where is it best to plant them? The authorities seem to differ in their opinion. W.R. Dykes, who was the great authority on irises, says that *Iris pumila* ought to be divided and transplanted every second year. He says they exhaust the soil. Yet I have grown a patch of them in a stone sink for some ten years and they have never flowered better than this year. The behaviour of plants is indeed inexplicable. It breaks all the rules; and that is what makes gardening so endlessly various and interesting.

I have come to the conclusion, after many years of sometimes sad experience, that you cannot come to any conclusion at all. But one simple thing I have discovered in gardening; a simple thing one never sees mentioned in gardening books. It is the fact that many plants do better if they can get their roots under stones. May I suggest that you might plant your little early irises into the cracks between paving or along the edges of a paved path, where they will not be walked on? I feel sure that

Iris pumila

this is the place to grow them, rather than down the front of a border, as is often recommended in books about gardening. They are not things for the herbaceous border: they are things for stone paths, surely; and the grey background of the paving enhances their delicacy of colouring. The worst that can be said against them is that they do not remain very long in flower, but they are so unobtrusive and take up so little room that their few weeks of flowering-life entitle them to a place where they can subsequently grow forgotten.

FLOWERING CURRANTS

The old flowering currant, *Ribes sanguineum*, is a familiar sight in cottage gardens, where it may sometimes be seen clipped into shape as a hedge, and a very dense, pretty hedge it makes, clothed at this time of year with a mass of pink flowers. A most reliable shrub, never taking a year off, and demanding the minimum of care or cultivation, it cannot lay claim to great distinction, and indeed some people despise the somewhat dingy pink of the individual flower; these people, with whom I find myself in agreement, should not be satisfied with the original type, introduced from the west of the United States in 1826, but should obtain its varieties 'Splendens' and 'King Edward VII', both far brighter in colour and just as accommodating in temperament.

I suppose that most people know the tip of cutting generous sheaves of the common flowering currant in January and putting them in a pail of water indoors, when they will come into flower by March, as purely white as any branch of the wild cherry?

There are, however, others less often seen. One of these is *Ribes speciosum*, which I can liken only to a prickly fuchsia. As cross and spiny as a gooseberry, this Californian dangles annually during April and May with quantities of miniature red fuchsia-like flowers, hung in rows of little tassels all along its reddish young shoots. If trained against a wall these shoots will stick out horizontally to a length of twelve or eighteen inches with very charming effect, especially if it can be planted where the sunlight will strike the shoots, turning them almost to the blood-red transparency of a cornelian or of a dog's pricking ear, backed by a bright light. It is not necessary to give it the protection of a wall, except in very cold districts, for it will grow quite happily as a bush in the open, but there is no doubt that it does make a very decorative wall-covering.

There is also *Ribes aureum*, which I find described in an old catalogue as the Buffalo Currant of the Wild West. The flowers, in this case, are yellow; and have the advantage, for those who like cloves, of diffusing that spicy scent, and there is the further advantage that the leaves in autumn will turn to a fine gold.

MAY

When skies are gentle, breezes bland,
When loam that's warm within the hand
Falls friable between the tines,
Sow hollyhocks and columbines,
The tufted pansy, and the tall
Snapdragon in the broken wall,
Not for this summer, but for next,
Since foresight is the gardener's text,
And though his eyes may never know
How lavishly his flowers blow,
Others will stand and musing say
"These were the flowers he sowed that May".

The Land

CARPETING

The more I prowl round my garden at this time of year, especially during that stolen hour of half-dusk between tea and supper, the more do I become convinced that a great secret of good gardening lies in covering every patch of the ground with some suitable carpeter. Much as I love the chocolate look of the earth in winter, when spring comes back I always feel that I have not done enough, not nearly enough, to plant up the odd corners with little low things that will crawl about, keeping weeds away, and tucking themselves into chinks that would otherwise be devoid of interest or prettiness.

The violets, for instance: I would not despise even our native *Viola odorata* of the banks and hedgerows, either in its blue or its white form, so well deserving its adjective *odorata*. And how it spreads, wherever it is happy, so why not let it roam and range as it listeth? (I defy any foreigner to pronounce that word.) There are other violets, more choice than our wilding; the little pink 'Coeur d'Alsace', or *Viola labradorica*, for instance, which from a few thin roots planted last year is now making huge clumps and bumps of purplish leaf and wine-coloured flower, and is sowing itself all over the place wherever it is wanted or not wanted. It is never not wanted, for it can be lifted and removed to another place, to spread at its good will.

There are many other carpeters beside the violets, some for sunny places and some for shade. For sunny places the thymes are perhaps unequalled, but the sunny places are never difficult to fill. Shady corners are more likely to worry the gardener trying to follow my advice of cram, cram, cram every chink and cranny. *Arenaria balearica* loves a dark, damp home, especially if it can be allowed to crawl adhesively

A view into the Rose Garden showing *Magnolia liliiflora* 'Nigra' and *Clematis montana* 'Rubens'.

Chaenomeles 'Boule de Feu' and
Malus hupehensis

over mossy stones. On a dark green mat it produces masses of what must be one of the tiniest flowers, pure white, starry; an easygoing jewel for the right situation. *Cotula squalida*, which ill deserves its name, is like a miniature fern, and it will spread widely and will help to keep the weeds away.

The acaenas will likewise spread widely, and should do well in shade; they have bronzy-coloured leaves and crawl neatly over their territory. The list of carpeters is endless, and I wish I had enough space to amplify these few suggestions. The one thing I feel sure of is that every odd corner should be packed wth something permanent, something of interest and beauty, something tucking itself into something else in the natural way of plants when they sow themselves and combine as we never could combine them with all our skill and knowledge.

IN YOUR HOUSE

Perhaps I should entitle this *Your Garden in Your House*, because I want to write something about cut flowers, inspired by an interesting letter from a gentleman describing himself as a botanist and horticulturist who has carried out researches on this very subject. This is the time of year when owners of gardens begin to pick more recklessly, with less dread of spoiling their outdoor show, but this pleasurable occupation does take a long time, and the busy woman wants to make her flowers last as long as possible.

"The cause of difficulties with cut flowers," says my correspondent, "lies in the entry of air into the water tubes of the flower stems during the period between cutting the flowers and placing them in water." To prevent such disappointment, he recommends that you should place your newly cut flowers in recently boiled water while it is still just above tepid, i.e., not hot enough to sting your hand but warm enough to give your fingers an agreeable sensation of warmth. Cut your flowers, he says, during dull, sunless hours; a recommendation that we have all found out for ourselves; but I wonder how many readers of this article are going to go wandering round with a kettle of recently boiled water? These things take time, and one has other things to do. Still, I shall try it.

My correspondent condemns as an old wives' tale the placing of aspirin tablets or copper coins in the water. He gives a slight approval to lumps of charcoal, in so far as they absorb air from the water. I suppose that we all have our theories, but this idea of air entering the stems is worth consideration. I pass it on to you.

I now return to the garden proper. Have you got _Viburnum carlcephalum_? If not, please get it at once. It is a hybrid of _Viburnum carlesii_, which we all know and grow, and it is a far better thing. Its head of flower is tighter and denser; its scent is stronger; and its habit is vigorous. My own plant is young and small; but I am told by people who have seen it growing fully developed that it makes a huge bush in the course of time. It is one of the most exciting things I have had in my garden for years past; not very exciting as to its colour, which is white flushed with pink in the bud; but most exciting as to its powerful scent. It is flowering now, April-May.

Halesia carolina, the snowdrop tree, is also just coming into flower. This is a very pretty flowering tree, seldom seen in gardens; it is hung with white, bell-shaped blossoms, among pale green leaves, all along the branches. It can be grown as a bush in the open, or trained against a wall. There is a better version of it, called _Halesia monticola_, but if you cannot obtain this from your nurseryman _Halesia carolina_ will do as well.

FLOWERING HEDGES

The problem of what hedge to plant round a new property is always with us.

Something rather more unusual may be found in _Chaenomeles japonica_, the cumbersome name under which our old friend _Pyrus japonica_ seems at last to have come to rest. This ornamental quince makes an extraordinarily pretty hedge, spurred right back to the old wood, and covered with flowers in April. The fruits of some varieties turn a rich burnished golden-pink in autumn, and may be used for making jelly if one has the heart to pick them off. _C. superba_ 'Boule de Feu', with vermilion flowers, is specially to be recommended for its fruits.

There is a wide choice as to colour in the flowers. The dark red _speciosa_ so often seen growing against old cottages is well known, but there is also a pale pink 'Moerloesii' and one appropriately called 'Apple Blossom', a strong coral-orange misnamed 'Knap Hill Scarlet', and a pure white, 'Nivalis'.

If you want something wickedly thorny, a real defence against cattle or little boys, try *C. cathayensis*. Its flowers are rather pale and insignificant, but its jade-green fruits of enormous size, bigger than a Jaffa orange, are most striking.

The Japanese quinces should be thinned-out after they have flowered, and to keep the hedge tidy may have their tips pinched back in August. It is worth mentioning that the Japanese quinces come surprisingly easily from seed. One single fruit will produce more seedlings than anybody could possibly make use of.

Prunus cerasifera, the myrobalan or cherry plum, makes a charming hedge, especially if kept pruned to a height which allows you to look down into the garnet-rid tips when the sun strikes them. They are then transparently luminous, as though they had a light behind them.

The drawback of this prunus used for hedging is that it tends to develop a "leg" or sturdy little trunk, with all the growth interlacing along the top, because its original intention was to shoot up into a tall tree: it thus cannot be described as dense towards the base, certainly not dense enough to prevent cats, dogs, or rabbits from squeezing through. Otherwise, its merits are great, for its flat top of young tips glows like a jewel.

The Chinese crab apple, *Malus hupehensis*, if left to itself, will grow into a tree between twenty and thirty feet high, but may be kept pruned to anything between six and eight feet, when it will form a curiously twisty, interweaving barrier of twiggy branches. Although deciduous, it thus remains reasonably dense in winter. In summer it is very dense indeed; in autumn the leaves colour well, and it retains its clusters of fruit well into the late autumn. The flower, which is white, is scented.

All this should be enough to recommend it, but it is further claimed that it will grow over a foot a year, and that within six years it will have gained all the appearance of an established hedge. It is not exorbitantly expensive, and should be planted at intervals of a foot and a half.

This is for a tall hedge, almost a wind break, but if you want something low and small, something which might take the place of edging box or dwarf lavender, here are two suggestions. *Berberis buxifolia* 'Nana', about two feet high, is evergreen with orange flowers. Clearly, this is not suitable for a boundary hedge, but it can look charming in the interior of the garden bordering a path or edging a border. It should be planted eighteen inches apart.

The other small shrub, about three feet high, forming a neatly rounded head covered with very fragrant pale-pink flowers in May and June is *Daphne burkwoodii* 'Somerset'. Many daphnes, as we know to our cost, have a way of dying off suddenly for no apparent reason, but *D*. 'Somerset' seems to be less given to this trick than most, and it is worth risking the loss of a plant in a bordering hedge for the sake of its scent, recalling one of its parents, the well-known *D. cneorum*. As the little bushes have a wide spread they can be planted two feet or more apart, so a few will go quite a long way. It is always wisest to get young plants where daphnes are concerned, and if in pots so much the better. They don't like disturbance. No less an authority than the then Director of Kew once said sternly to me: "Never let a daphne see a spade".

If you happen to have a stretch inside the garden where you wish to cut off one area from another, say the kitchen garden from the lawn or from the flower garden, and can afford the space for a fairly loose hedge, i.e., not closely clipped, consider the claims of *Osmanthus delavayi*. It is usually seen growing as a single specimen bush, but makes a strong and uncommon hedge, especially useful if you need something for a west aspect where other things might not flower so well. Above all, it is evergreen.

Finally, for the enterprising, a mixed hedge is something not often seen. You can have it practically evergreen by planting holly, yew, tree box, larch, beech, and copper beech, all mixed together. Larch is of course deciduous, and the two beeches are marcescent, meaning that they retain their brown leaves until the spring growth pushes them off, but the holly, yew, and tree box will suffice for the evergreen effect throughout the winter. It takes some patience to grow a hedge of this type, but the years go by quicker than one thinks and in the end the solid patchwork wall is most rewarding.

Daphne burkwoodii

TROUBLE-FREE STRIPS

There is often a strip of ground in a garden which cannot be put to good purpose without more labour than we can devote to it. It may once have been a lawn, which means mowing; or a long border, which needs weeding and upkeep; or merely a strip along the boundary fence in a hitherto uncultivated garden, which demands some treatment to turn it into something better than a rough waste. I had an idea for such a place, which should be both pretty and labour-saving.

The shape does not matter so very much; it could be rectangular, square, or even circular, though I fancy a long narrow rectangle would give the best effect. What is important is that it should be *flat*, and that the ground surface should be level. You then plant it at regular intervals (say fifteen feet apart either way) with young stripling sapling trees, straight of stem and twiggy of head; it will be important to keep the stems clean of growth so that you can always see through and between them. A thin little grove is what I have in mind. The silver birch with its pale bark would be ideal, especially in a light or sandy soil; the lime, or linden, for any soil; the whitebeam, whose underside leaves show silver in the breeze; and even young oaks, round-topped and grown as standards.

The question will then arise of what you plant underneath. Since the heads of the little trees will be very green, the accent should be on emphasising the greenness. Turf is probably impossible, because of the mowing, and anyway I think one should aim at a brighter green than that. I have a great weakness for sweet woodruff; it does not object to shade, it remains green from April until the autumn, it can be grown

Pieris forrestii

from seed, and it would make a dense cushion rather like those enormous eiderdowns that one finds in old-fashioned French hotels. I would also plant some patches of greenish flowers; for instance, the green and silver Star-of-Bethlehem, *Ornithogalum nutans*; our native wood anemone; lily-of-the-valley; and, for later in the year, some clumps of Solomon's seal and the sweet-smelling *Smilacina racemosa*. I am not quite sure about these: they might be too tall, and might interrupt the vistas between the straight little trunks. Obviously such planting must depend upon individual taste, but of one thing I feel sure; that all colour must be excluded. It must all be green and white; cool, symmetrical, and severe.

*B*LAZING PIERIS

This is to recommend a shrub startling to the eye in spring, for it presents the richest reddest coloration of autumn. People blink in unbelief when they first see the dark green bush tipped with vivid scarlet. They mistake the poinsettia-red tips for an inflorescence, but on going closer, discover that they are in fact the young shoots of leaves, fiery, pointed, glossy, and looking as though they had some artificial lighting behind them.

This is *Pieris forrestii*, named after George Forrest, who first found it growing wild in the Yunnan province of China.

Of all the pierises, Forrest's is the most magnificent. *Pieris japonica* is good enough, but Forrest's far excels it. He must have been surprised when he came across it blazing on the slopes of its native mountains. The nib of Farrer's pen would have struck such sparks as to kindle his whole page into a bonfire. Unfortunately, Forrest lacked the descriptive powers of Reginald Farrer, and is content to remark merely that it is "a most excellent shrub", finer than any of its class he has seen. It was first shown at Chelsea in 1924, so is a fairly recent acquisition for our gardens.

I have expatiated on the beauty of the young shoots, which indeed is the glory of this plant, but the flowers also have their charm. They come in hanging clusters of creamy little bells, at the same time as the young shoots, so that the whole plant in April or May gives an effect of dark green, bright red, and pale tassels.

It has its drawbacks — what plant hasn't? Belonging as it does to the botanical family of the *Ericaceae*, it is a lime-hater. You can grow it safely in any soil where rhododendrons, azaleas, or kalmias flourish, or you can make up a peaty bed for it with lots of leaf mould, but it will have nothing to say to an alkaline or chalky soil. Another of its dislikes is cold winds and who shall blame it? Finally, it dislikes late spring frosts, but again who shall blame it? We can, however, arrange to protect our plants better than we can arrange to protect ourselves: we have to move about, whatever the weather, whereas our plants are static and it is up to us, their masters, to place them in the position that suits them best. A hurdle stuffed with straw or bracken will do much to defend them against the prevailing wind. Many of us would have been glad to cower, during the early weeks of May this year, behind so kind and cosy a stockade.

THE MOUTAN TREE PAEONY

The Moutan tree paeony, *Paeonia suffruticosa*, is surely one of the most handsome shrubs we possess. It has been known and grown in this country ever since 1787 or 1789, anyhow since the time of the French Revolution, yet how seldom is it seen except in the garden of the connoisseur?

I must put a brake on my pen lest I become too lyrical about it. But, really, why should one timidly repress one's enthusiasms? I feel sure that anyone would agree, who had seen my one plant last May, carrying two dozen enormous flowers detectable by their scent twenty yards away. It is, I suppose, about eight years old now, and every year it increases in vigour and in the number of those great splendid blooms, the size of soup plates, white with a purple centre so delicately tapered away into hair-strokes that might have been drawn up by a sable paint-brush.

Two dozen flowers did I say? I should not boast. Sir Abraham Hume, of Wormleybury in Hertfordshire, in 1826 had a plant seven feet high, forty feet in circumference, and carrying 660 buds.

P. suffruticosa comes from China, Tibet and Bhutan. It has a large progeny of hybrids, for it will cross with other species such as *P. lutea*, so there is a wide range of colour to choose from, in rose-pink, purple, crimson, salmon, maroon. Personally I ask for nothing better than the original wild Moutan before the hybridisers had started interfering with it, but there is no denying that some of its crosses are extremely beautiful. A list of over two score named varieties can be obtained from nurserymen who specialise in them. You may have to pay a guinea and more for a two-year-old plant, but as that plant will probably outlive you it can scarcely be regarded as a bad investment. In China, evidently, the price of a paeony root went according to age. Writing in the ninth century A.D., the Chinese poet Po Chü-i says:

> The cost of the plant depends on the number of blossoms.
> For the fine flower, a hundred pieces of damask;
> For the cheap flower, five bits of silk.

The plants you receive will in all probability be grafted, and in order to avoid a crop of undesirable suckers you should be careful to set the graft below the soil level. This will ensure the plant getting eventually on to its own roots.

The tree paeony should be placed where the sun will not strike it until the morning is well advanced. It is said in fact that it will thrive in a north aspect; this seems rather drastic treatment, and I would prefer to see it in slight shade in the open, perhaps facing west.

A SECRET FOR ARUMS

People who still treasure some arum lilies in pots under glass for the sake of those swan-like flowers looking as though they came out of a Hans Andersen story may now be wondering what to do with them. The orthodox treatment is to stand them out in a frame or to tip them into a trench, and let them rest until the time comes to start them into growth again in late summer.

I suggest that anybody who has a potful to spare might try the experiment of knocking them out of their pot and sinking them into a pond or pool, in much the same way as you would sink water-lilies, preferably in a wire-basket container whose mesh will allow the roots to escape downwards into the succulent mud below. It is rather surprising to see an arum lily flowering in water out-of-doors in an English summer. We associate them usually with Christmas or Easter, in florists' shops at a high price, and do not regard them as a possibility of our own, growing as they grow like weeds in the ditches of Morocco and Ethiopia. The botanical name of what we call the arum lily is *Zantedeschia aethiopica*, and as I have often said before, the weeds of other countries are the imported treasure-trove of ours.

If you think anything of this idea of growing the arum lily in a pool or pond, let me add some practical advice. You must realise that its tubers must be sunk deep enough to escape the freezing of the top layer of water during our harsh northern winters. It is unusual for ice to form more than six inches thick, so a plant sunk six inches deep below the water-level ought to escape the freezing danger overhead. It would be safer to sink it even deeper, say twelve inches.

If the idea of risking a precious pot of arums does not appeal to you, and if you just want to grow them on in the orthodox way, let me pass on a tip which was given to me by a countryman who grew some of the finest arums I ever saw. I suspected he had a deep secret which he wouldn't divulge. It took me a long time to worm it out of him. "Use your old tomato soil," he said at last, "the old soil you chuck out of the pots you've grown tomatoes in. Nothing better for arums. But don't tell anybody, will you?"

WILD FRITILLARIES

There was a note in this paper recently about our native fritillary, *Fritillaria meleagris*, and indeed this must rank as one of the most delightful wild flowers to introduce into our gardens. I notice that people always admire a small patch I have in an orchard, but by no means everybody knows what it is. It looks its best in grass, which is its natural home, but can also look charmingly graceful springing up

The azalea border in full flower.

amongst the stones of a rock garden. Where it is happy, it increases rapidly by self-sown seed, though of course it takes about four years for the new little bulbs to attain maturity.

A close examination of the turf will reveal the presence of seedlings not yet old enough to flower; they have a curious habit of lying flat to the ground when they first come through, looking as angular as a stick-insect and suggesting that a foot has trodden on them and snapped them, but after a few days they lift themselves into their normal erect position.

It has been observed, with no explanation so far as I know, that the white form predominates in cultivation, although in nature the white form appears relatively seldom amongst the dusky wine-colour of the type. Some growers have even suggested that a flower of the normal colour will reappear as a white flower after some seasons. It would be interesting to mark the position of some bulbs, and see if this really happens.

ON A NORTH WALL

A north wall, which gets no sun at all, is always something of a problem, whether it be the high wall of an old walled garden or merely the back of a house.

I have found the Morello cherry an admirable solution for such a situation. Not only is it foamingly pretty with its pure white blossom in April, but the bright red fruits, hanging in pairs like earrings are most decorative later. By the time they are ripe enough for use in pies or jam, they will have turned almost black and the birds will start stripping them.

To give them a good start, it is advisable and even essential to provide some support for fastening the branches back against the wall. Vine-eyes threaded with fairly stout wire will do, in horizontal strands a couple of feet apart, or wooden slats. Some people tie the shoots tightly back, each one separately, cutting out all superfluities, but although I do appreciate the sight of a beautifully, symmetrically trained fruit-tree, like the ribs of a fan, I have come to the belief that the Morello cherry looks even more attractive if left to grow a bit wildly, with the wands of blossom spraying forward as they will.

I might mention by the way that each cherry tree, fully grown and spread out, covers a wall space 21 ft wide and 20 ft high.

At the foot of the wall, where we naturally had to dig a long, narrow border for planting the cherries in the first instance, Nature

Fritillaria meleagris

has intervened with an arrangement I might never have thought of. A stray columbine seeded itself, and now the border is full of columbines of every variety, the aquilegia family being extremely promiscuous and inventive in its inter-hybridisation. There are the old granny's bonnets in their dusty pink or dark blue, and the lighter long-spurred hybrids in bright pink, yellow, mauve, white, crimson, copper. I think I must deliberately add some of the blue one called 'Hensol Harebell', which is not quite so tall and would come in usefully at the front of the border.

Had I thought out what to plant, before Nature took this very welcome hand, I suppose I would have gone in for some of the things one conventionally associates with shade – the old-fashioned dicentra or bleeding heart, Solomon's seal, or that shamefully neglected, heavily-scented relation of Solomon's seal, *Smilacina racemosa*, the creamy, feathery false spikenard, and perhaps some hostas with their grand leaves as an edging. But how much gayer and more unexpected the dancing columbines that, like humming birds, seem as though they belonged to the sun.

*T**HE ANSWER FOR ANEMONES***
So many people have recently remarked to me, "We cannot get anemones to do, whereas with you they seem to grow like weeds", that I began to wonder what the explanation could be, and have come to the conclusion that they do not get planted at the right time. In other words, the little black tuber of

Aquilegia hybrida

the anemone hates being kept out of the ground for longer than need be. It sometimes may linger in a paper bag until you have time to plant it, and furthermore, goodness knows how long it has been on its way between the nurseryman's garden and yours. Like impatient persons, it is annoyed by being kept waiting, but unlike impatient persons, it takes a suitable revenge by merely withering and dying. How distressing it would be if such were the reactions of our friends and acquaintances whenever we were late for an appointment.

There must be some curious philological or Grimm's Law which makes English-speaking people call anemones anenomes, transferring the *m* into the place of the *n*. So perhaps it is better to adopt the pretty though unscientific name of windflower, as it is about the anemones or windflowers that I want to write on this day of spring.

How gay they are, how brilliantly gay, how shiny, how variegated in their colours, these windflowers that come to us from different parts of the world. The season starts for us from Greece, with the starry blue *Anemone blanda*, flowering in March; succeeded by *A. apennina*, the equally starry and even more intensely blue Italian. Then there is the well-known double or semi-double 'St. Brigid', on sale everywhere early in the year, but to my mind greatly excelled by the 'De Caen', or poppy-flowered single; and excelled above all by the single, starry, 'St. Bavo'. This is the one I ardently want to commend to your attention at the moment.

I cannot imagine why people don't grow *Anemone* 'St. Bavo' more generously. It is cheap to buy a dozen of those little tubers which one doesn't know which way up to plant and it doesn't seem to matter anyhow – English as she is wrote. 'St. Bavo' is a hybrid of *Anemone coronaria*, and comes up in a range of colouring equalled by very few other easy flowers. Any description of the various colours would sound, on paper, like an exaggeration: wine-velvet with an electric-blue centre; scarlet with a black centre; pink or lilac with a biscuit-coloured centre; or a particularly subtle variety, which is like a ripe apricot hanging in the sun. At least, I thought it was, but when with a conscientious qualm I went back to have another look at it, I found I had been quite wrong. It was more as though you had pounded some old Tudor bricks into a paste, varnished the paste, and then shredded it into pointed petals.

*M*EMORIES OF MAY

There is nothing like the gentle, removing touch of slight illness to induce meditation over some experience recently enjoyed. One must not be too ill, only just ill enough to justify a couple of days in bed, with sufficient fever to heighten the perceptions. Life is laid aside; one is vaguely aware of a wood pigeon cooing in the distance; the tap of a thrush on a snail; the rustle of the breeze through poplars; all things very small but significant. In these moments, these brief dedicated hours with leisure enforced, one may ruminate as vacantly as a cow recumbent in her meadow.

In such a mood, I remembered going down into the wood to dig up some roots of a specially deep pink anemone. I had observed it growing there, and I knew from previous experience that if you are so fortunate as to discover a coloured anemone occurring amongst the white ones, you can transplant it with every hope that it will come up again in the same colour in your own garden. Vandals ignorantly dig up wild plants, at the wrong time, and treat them in such a way that they can never be expected to survive. I knew that I was doing right by my pink windflower in transplanting it to my garden. There was so much of it that it could well afford me a trowel-full of its roots.

That trowel-full of woodland soil taught me a lesson. It was so tightly crammed with growing things, all struggling for existence. Only a trowel, to disturb four square inches of ground in an English wood! There was a potential oak-tree, sprouting from an acorn. There were young brambles, already in their innocence threatening invasion. There were young honeysuckles, inch high, preparing to hoist themselves towards the light with the twiggy support of the hazel coppice. All a living tangle underground, struggling together, and me the superior human with my sharp weapon, prising up the chosen plant I wanted, destroying all that other scrambling and wrestling life, which might have come to completion had I not interfered.

Lying feverish in my bed I wondered whether I had done wrong or right. A whole crop of moral tangles came up. I had frustrated a young oak, but I had preserved a pink windflower. Where was the answer to be found in virtue?

All I knew was that the memory of that wood full of bluebells on a May morning would remain with me for ever.

*M*ORE MODEST IRISES

Amidst all the pomp and grandeur of oncoming June, some charming modest little irises blow almost unperceived. They are *Iris innominata, Iris douglasiana, Iris graminea,* and *Iris japonica.* Let me take them in order.

Iris innominata comes from the north-western States of America. It is no more than six or eight inches high, flowering amongst grass-like leaves, and it varies in colour from pale lilac, dark lilac, a pale pink, a pale buff, to a deep buff or a bronze. A variation full of interest; and an ideal pet for a pocket in the rock-garden. It can be grown from seed, an experi-

Anemone coronaria 'St Brigid' and 'De Caen'

ment which would demand the usual patience but might easily produce some interesting hybrids. It is said to like leaf mould and sand, a moist position, and semi-shade. I have it growing in ordinary garden soil, bone dry, in full sun, and it couldn't be flowering more extravagantly. Perhaps it will flower itself to death, but at the moment it shows no such intention.

Iris douglasiana somewhat resembles it. I have not got it, so cannot speak of it from personal experience, but I have seen it at shows and elsewhere, when I determined that it was a *must have*. This, again, produces many hybrid forms and can be grown from seed.

Iris graminea I do possess, and grow less for the garden value of its pinky-mauve flowers, almost hidden at the base of the leaf-clump, than for its curious scent like a sun-warmed greengage. It is essentially a little iris for picking, and can be seen very prettily marked once you have sorted it out from its leaves and can observe it closely in a glass or vase.

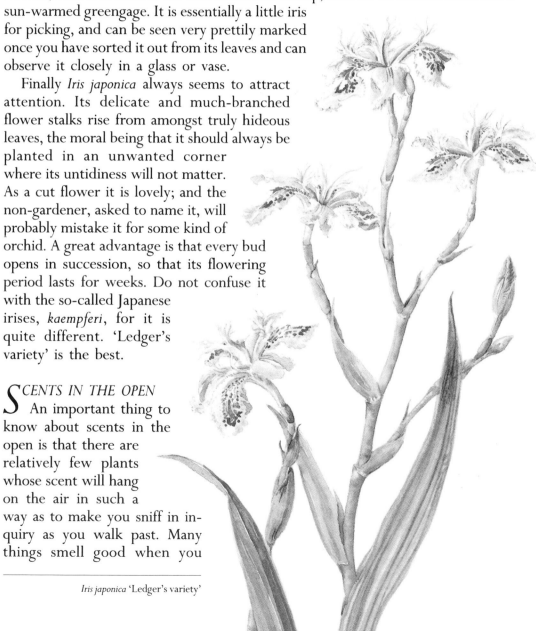

Finally *Iris japonica* always seems to attract attention. Its delicate and much-branched flower stalks rise from amongst truly hideous leaves, the moral being that it should always be planted in an unwanted corner where its untidiness will not matter. As a cut flower it is lovely; and the non-gardener, asked to name it, will probably mistake it for some kind of orchid. A great advantage is that every bud opens in succession, so that its flowering period lasts for weeks. Do not confuse it with the so-called Japanese irises, *kaempferi*, for it is quite different. 'Ledger's variety' is the best.

SCENTS IN THE OPEN

An important thing to know about scents in the open is that there are relatively few plants whose scent will hang on the air in such a way as to make you sniff in-quiry as you walk past. Many things smell good when you

Iris japonica 'Ledger's variety'

push your nose into them, or crush them, or bring them into a warm room, but what we are thinking about is the garden path as we stroll, something that will really hit you in surprise. I think my choice would be:

An edging of Cheddar pinks.
A hedge of hybrid musk roses, especially 'Penelope'.
Some bushes of the rugosa rose, 'Blanc double de Coubert'.
Azaleas.
A hedge of sweetbriar.
The Balsam poplar when it first unfolds its sticky leaves.
Lilium auratum, as a luxury.
Humea elegans, the incense plant, another luxury because it has to be raised in heat and planted out for the summer.

I know everyone will disagree and everyone will have other ideas of his own. I quite expect a spate of suggestions about the things I have left out, for in the region of the five senses the sense of smell (and the allied sense of taste) is highly controversial. Some people love the scent of phlox: to me, it suggests pig-stys, not that I dislike pig-stys, being country-born, and well accustomed to them. Much depends also on the keenness of the nose, and also on the fact that not all scented plants give off their scent all the time. They may vary with the temperature, with the degree of moisture in the air, and even with the time of day. This capriciousness makes them perhaps more precious. One may catch an unexpected whiff as one passes a bush of winter sweet or witch hazel, not to be detected an hour ago, or of that vanilla-scented little tree, *Azara microphylla*. And the scent of box in the sun, and of box-clippings as you crush them underfoot. And of a bed of warm wallflowers. And the night-scented stock, that lack-lustre annual which comes into its own after twilight.

But perhaps there is nothing to equal the woodland acres of our native bluebell, smoke-blue as an autumn bonfire, heavy in scent as a summer rose, yet young as the spring which is its season.

JUNE

June of the iris and the rose.
The rose not English as we fondly think.
Anacreon and Bion sang the rose;
And Rhodes the isle whose very name means rose
Struck roses on her coins . . .
The Young Crusaders found the Syrian rose
Springing from Saracenic quoins,
And China opened her shut gate
To let her roses through, and Persian shrines
Of poetry and painting gave the rose.

The Garden

ABUNDANT ROSES

One is almost compelled to write about roses at this time of year. One sets out with the intention of writing about something else, and then one's pen takes charge because one has suddenly noticed some rose whose beauty has come to maturity and is doing its stuff as it never did before.

Such a rose is *Rosa odorata gigantea*. Perhaps I ought hastily to say that it is rather a plant for the connoisseur. By this I don't mean that it is tender or in any need of special care. I mean simply that it doesn't make a great splash of effect, and I mean also that you have to wait three or four years before it starts to flower in earnest. When it does start, it behaves generously; there is nothing stingy about its giving.

It is a white rose, single, with a quivering knob of brown stamens in the middle. A very vigorous climber, with glossy dark foliage. I fancy that it would look well if allowed to grow up an old tree where it could hang loosely and disperse its scent on the breeze, for, as its name reveals, it is powerfully scented. This method would also dispose of the drawback of having to wait, wasting valuable wall space, until such time as it decided to flower. Placed at the foot of a tree, it could be left to itself, climbing yearly higher and higher in preparation for the day when a swarm of huge white butterflies is apparently about to take flight into the upper air.

Another rose which is perfectly adapted to a similar position is *R. moschata floribunda*, the musk rose of the Himalayas. This will grow anything up to 30 feet and more, and I leave you to imagine its scent. This, again, is white, with clusters of many small flowers, but if you don't care over much for too many white flowers in the garden, lovely though these tall climbers look in a moonlit orchard, try *R. multiflora*

Climbing *Hydrangea petiolaris* overhanging the iron gate which leads from the entrance courtyard to the Rose Garden *cathayensis*, a pale, delicate pink. There is in fact no end to the climbing roses which may be used in this way, not forgetting the old 'Félicité et Perpetué' which some people call (I think mistakenly) the 'Seven Sisters' rose.

If you want something really alarming in its vigour, get *R. filipes*, but be sure to obtain the 'Kiftsgate' variety. Anyone who has seen this in the lovely garden of Kiftsgate Court, Chipping Campden, where it originated and where it now spreads over a horizontal span of about 50 feet, must have gasped at the possibilities offered by such a rose. It will go sideways, or up. In my own garden it smothers a moribund almond. The almond may resent it, but I don't, since the sparrows pick all the buds off the almond and never a pink flower do I get, so I just use the poor almond as a host and let *R. filipes* drape it in veils of white lace towards the end of June or beginning of July.

VIRGINIAN COWSLIP

Mentally surveying some of the delights of spring, which are already over, I recalled with gratitude the Virginian cowslip, *Mertensia virginica*. Some American visitors, strolling round my garden, stopped to gaze at it in distrustful surprise. To them it was a weed, and for a moment I thought they were going to show their helpfulness by pulling it up. Thus do we often fail to remember that the treasures of our own gardens are the weeds of other lands. The Japanese, after all, always ate the bulbs of *Lilium auratum*, scale by scale, after the manner of a globe artichoke, until they discovered that the European market esteemed the wild bulb of Mount Fujiyama for its flower.

My Americans had just been enraptured by their first sight of an English bluebell wood; and when I remarked that the mertensia smothering its native woodland must be every whit as beautiful, they gaped at me as though I had said something paradoxical. They evidently thought me daft for cherishing six poor plants of a thing they were accustomed to see growing by the acre. My pleasure in my mertensia was not thereby diminished. A lovely sky-blue with grey-green leaves, it had been flowering for weeks, from the middle of April right up to the end of May, in the broken light of a corner under some cobnuts, for although it will thrive equally well in sun it is one of those useful things which really prefer the shade. What it does insist on is a loose, leafy soil with some sand, or a peaty soil; and since the 2 foot stems are rather brittle, it is advisable to support them with a few twiggy sticks, otherwise they flop and sometimes snap. Do not be alarmed if it starts to look very miserable in June. It is not dead, but merely dying down according to its nature. It will reappear next year.

I cannot imagine why the Americans should call it a cowslip. Cowslips, as we all know, are yellow, and belong to the great family of primulas, whereas the mertensia of Virginia is as blue as our own naturalised comfrey, and indeed belongs to the same botanical family as the comfrey, the *Boraginaceae*. Do you grow comfrey? A terrible spreader, but so refreshingly blue when the skies of June are grey. It makes a good successor to the mertensia, for a blue corner, and, like the mertensia, does not mind a shady site. It is well named *peregrinum*, the pilgrim or walker, for it walks about all

Mertensia virginica

over the place. You can always tear it up if it becomes too invasive, leaving just a patch of the size you want.

A HARMONIOUS ROSE
It is time I mentioned *Rosa rubrifolia*, a species native to the Alps and the Pyrenees, and over parts of Central Europe as far east as Yugoslavia. I have never seen it growing in the wild; I should like to.

I can imagine its smooth reddish stems and grey-green foliage sprouting amongst rocks aromatic with lavender, rosemary, thyme, and cistus, all hot and scented under a southern summer sun. We cannot reproduce these conditions in our damp island gardens. But we can grow *Rosa rubrifolia*, and we should and could and must.

It has so many virtues. I enumerate them: it is completely hardy. It has this unusual colouring of its red thornless stem, and its graceful habit of arching itself about, growing very tall, seven to eight or nine feet, which makes it a very valuable shrub rose for a border or for a specimen plant in the corner of a lawn.

The flowers do not amount to much, in the estimation of people who prefer huge vulgar blooms such as the famous 'Peace'. The flower of *Rosa rubrifolia* is tiny, pink, pretty, insignificant. The beauty of the plant lies in its foliage and its way of growth, and perhaps also in the eye of the beholder, a very important thing for any fastidious gardener.

This rose, *rubrifolia*, is easy to come by. People often write to me asking where they can obtain the plants I recommend. They seem to think I keep a deep, dark secret, but I always answer, I hope by return of post, any inquiry from readers. I do try to.

The two plants of *Rosa rubrifolia* I have got in my own garden are young and immature. I look forward to the day, perhaps two summers hence, when they will have grown up into the size they should be – huge, wild, plum-coloured tossing sprays, curving over a planting of iris called 'Rosy Wings', which is just the same colour and flowers at the same time.

PAEONIES FROM SEED

Surely I must have written before now about the leisurely pleasure of growing species paeonies from seed. Leisurely because it takes four to five years before they start to flower; pleasure because you never know exactly what is going to turn up, and may get slight but interesting variations. Some seed I took from a rather dull maroon-coloured *P. delavayi* produced a child of lacquer red. With the usual perversity of plants, the parent survives and has grown far too large for the position I gave it; a chaffinch has nested in it, which is very charming, but I never dreamt it would grow eight foot high; the child, which I felt really proud of, succumbed without warning, probably to the disease commonly called wilt. This disease, caused by a fungus, is infectious and plants attacked by it should be destroyed.

The lovely pale yellow *P. mlokosewitschii* also varies slightly in the colour of its offspring. I got a greenish-yellow one from the butter-yellow parent. These two happy accidents should suffice to confirm my contention that it is worth while growing the species from your own saved seed, or from a packet of purchased seed. By the way, do not confuse the species with the old herbaceous paeony of borders and cottage gardens. The species are far more subtle and exquisite. If they have a fault, it is that their flowers are more ephemeral. You can obviate this to a considerable extent by setting your plants in broken shade, for a hot sun will cook the flower quickly. Luckily, they prefer broken shade, and this alone makes them desirable as an under-planting for a grove of small standard trees such as the ornamental pyrus and prunus, where the ground might otherwise remain bare and without interest after the blossom of the trees has gone over.

I should recommend the pale sorts rather than the magenta colours. The pale, ghostly, papery

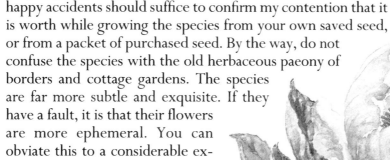

Paeonia mlokosewitschii

flowers of *P. wittmanniana, lactiflora* 'Whitleyi Major', *obovata,* and the white *emodi* all suggest moonlight at midday. The magenta ones are, to my thinking, too strong to mix with the wraiths.

PURPLE PLANTING

If one has a garden large enough to afford the space, it is interesting to devote a section to flowers of a special colour. I have tried this experiment myself, and although I must admit that it sounds better on paper than it looks in practice, I still maintain that the idea is a good one.

I have for instance a square white-and-grey garden, which is really quite successful, cool with lilies and white roses and grey-foliaged plants on a summer evening, and another separate enclosure where all the hot colours of red and yellow and orange are segregated and concentrated, on the theory that these colours are difficult to place unless kept to themselves.

But this is by the way. It is about a border ranging through the pale mauves up to the rich imperial purples that I wish to write. I can't honestly say that it has come off, as yet, according to my vision in the imagination; one's planting dreams seldom do, but one lives in the hope of improving year after year. Should any reader wish to know my scheme, here it is.

In the foreground, purple pansies such as *Viola* 'Ullswater' or 'Huntercombe Purple', raised from seed. Lumps of lavender, the dwarf *Lavendula spica* 'Hidcote' (*nana atropurpurea*) and *L. stoechas* which is far hardier than usually supposed. All these come towards the front. Between them, to fill up gaps in spring, I have tulips, such as the reliable old Darwin 'Bishop' and the striped white-and-purple 'Habit de Noce'. The tall *Allium rosenbachianum* towers in a great mop-head behind them. A few irises contribute their purple to the colour scheme.

Later on, *Thalictrum dipterocarpum*, the meadow rue, comes up in its feathery spires, and there are lumps of that old herbaceous stand-by, *Salvia nemorosa* 'virgata', so hardy as to be almost indestructible. *Campanula glomerata* comes in usefully, with its fat head of a really deep purple. Petunias fill up the gaps, helpful annuals, but annuals are only temporary things, and although they make a show for the summer display they can hold no permanent interest.

Thus, I have tried to introduce the deep purple clematis into my border, 'Gipsy Queen' and other *jackmanii* hybrids. One can train them over a framework of wooden slats, flattening them out, as on a table-top, if one has not got a wall to train them up, or they can be grown up a triangle of wooden stakes.

I have also planted a few delphiniums at the back of my purple border. They are bright blue, but I think the blue combines well with the purple scheme, and somehow enhances the colour. A painter friend of mine, who besides being a painter is also a far better gardener than I, does not agree. She says purple and blue quarrel together.

She may be right. All I know is that my purple border is not yet the success I meant it to be, but that I shall struggle on with it until I get it into something worth looking at.

BATH GARDENS

I know a man who collects baths. He buys broken-down baths for a few shillings at local auction sales and buries them in his garden, with the waste-hole open and a thick layer of coke clinker or some similar rough stuff underneath to ensure drainage. He then fills the bath up to the rim with whatever kind of soil he requires; covers the rim over; and there he is, with a securely insulated patch in which to grow his choosy plants.

I am not suggesting that our gardens should all become a submerged cemetery for obsolete baths, but it does seem to me a helpful idea for people who have a difficult soil to cope with, people who want to grow things that will not consent to flourish in the soil they have been blessed or cursed with. The dwellers on chalk, for example, who wish to grow the lime-hating *Gentiana sino-ornata*, could overcome their difficulty. The dwellers on clay would find that the indestructible, uncontrollable clay could be suppressed in favour of a soft bed suitable to peat-loving subjects.

Again, if you want a swampy bit of ground for moisture-loving primulas, you can create it, very suitably, in the buried bath. Again, if you have a flinty soil, which throws up flints over and over from the bottom, however often you may think you have cleared them out, you can replace that spiteful bit of ground with a richer loam, controlled and contained within the rectangular shape of the sunken bath. It is an idea lending itself to much expansion.

Meanwhile I have been deriving much pleasure from a June-flowering garlic called *Allium albopilosum*. A native of Turkestan, it comes up in a large mop-sized head of numerous perfectly star-shaped flowers of sheeny lilac, each with a little green button at the centre, on long thin stalks, so that the general effect is of a vast mauve-and-green cobweb, quivering with its own lightness and buoyancy. They can be bought quite cheaply, but even a group of six makes a fine show.

Quite easy to grow, they prefer a light soil and a sunny place, and may be increased to any extent by the little bulbils which form round the parent bulb, a most economical way of multiplying your stock. They would mix very happily with the blue *Allium caeruleum*, sometimes called *A. azureum*, in front of them. These are cheaper, not quite so tall, and overlap in their flowering season, thus prolonging the display.

THYME LAWNS

Two years ago, in 1948, I had what I thought might be a bright idea. It has turned out so bright, in both senses of the word, that I must pass it on.

I had two small windswept beds (the size was eight yards long by five yards wide each), divided by a path of paving stones down the middle. I tried every sort of thing in them, including a mad venture of hollyhocks, which, of course, got flattened by the prevailing south-west wind, however strongly we staked them. So then I decided I must have something very low-grading, which would not suffer from the wind, and scrapped the hollyhocks, and dibbled in lots and lots of the common thyme, and now have a sort of lawn which, while it is densely flowering in purple and red, looks like a Persian carpet laid flat on the ground out of doors. The bees think that I have laid it for their especial benefit. It really is a lovely sight; I do not want to boast, but I cannot help being pleased with it; it is so seldom that one's experiments in gardening are wholly successful.

I have planted a few bulbs of small things in amongst the thyme, to give some interest in the spring when the thyme is merely green. A patch of crocuses; a patch of the miniature narcissus; a patch of the little pink cyclamen. It occurs to me also that if you have not a flat bed to devote to a thyme lawn you could fill a sunny bank with it. Steep grass banks are always awkward to mow, but the thyme would not need any mowing, and it should revel in a sunny exposure with the good drainage of a slope. You might plant some of the rock-roses, or sun-roses, hybrids of *Helianthemum nummularium*, amongst the thyme; these sun-roses can be obtained in a variety of brilliant colours, ranging from pale buff and yellow to tomato pink and deep red, and they flower for at least six weeks during May and June.

COLOUR PLANNING

I have a gardening dodge which I find very useful. It concerns colour schemes and plant groupings. You know how quickly one forgets what one's garden has looked like during different weeks progressively throughout the year? One makes a mental note, or even a written note, and then the season changes and one forgets what one meant at the time. One has written "Plant something yellow near the yellow tulips", or "Plant something tall behind the lupins", and then autumn comes and plants have died down, and one scratches one's head trying to remember what on earth one meant by that.

My system is more practical. I observe, for instance, a great pink, lacy crinoline of the May-flowering tamarisk, of which I put in two snippets years ago, and which now spreads the exuberance of its petticoats twenty feet wide over a neglected corner of the garden. What could I plant near it to enhance its colour? It must, of course, be something which will flower at the same time. So I try effects, picking flowers elsewhere, rather in the way that one makes a flower arrangement in the house, sticking them into the ground and then standing back to observe the harmony. The dusky, rosy *Iris* 'Senlac' is just

Allium christophii

the right colour; I must split up my clumps as soon as they have finished flowering and make a group of those near the tamarisk for next May. The common pink columbine, almost a weed, would do well for underplanting, or some pink pansies, 'Crimson Queen', or the wine-red shades, as a carpet; and for something really noble, the giant foxtail lily, *Eremurus robustus*, eight to ten feet high. I cut, with reluctance, one precious spike from a distant group, and stick it in; it looks fine, like a cathedral spire flushed warm in the sunset. Undoubtedly I must have some eremuri next year with the plumy curtains of the tamarisk behind them.

This is just one example. One feels like an artist painting a picture – putting in a dash of colour here, taking out another dash of colour there, until the whole composition is to one's liking, and at least one knows exactly what effect will be produced twelve months hence.

To conclude, may I recommend planting tamarisk? It is graceful, hardy, and no bother. You can control its size by hard pruning, if necessary, though for my own part I like to see it growing as it listeth. *T. pentandra* flowers in August and September; *T. tetrandra* is the one I have been writing about, and flowers in May. *T. gallica* flowers in late summer and does particularly well by the sea, where it can be used as a windbreak. They all strike easily from cuttings in autumn.

*T*HYME AGAIN

About nine years ago, to be exact on June 18, 1950, I wrote about two little lawns I had planted with thyme, the creeping *Thymus serpyllum*, the sort commonly used between paving stones.

This idea was taken up by quite a lot of readers and I believe reproduced in corners of their own gardens. After so long a lapse of time, it may be permissible to return with a few comments on the mistakes I made and such success as I achieved.

Mistakes first. It was an error to plant some small bulbs amongst the thyme. I had put in crocuses, and fritillaries, and some corms of the autumn cyclamen. They grew all right and loved being where they were, but they made the thyme lawn look untidy by breaking the flatness. They have now been eliminated and replanted elsewhere. The thyme lawn looks much better without them.

Another mistake I made was to mix a white variety with the red and purple thymes. This made it look too patchy. A carpet of only red and purple and mauve would have been more homogeneous. Or so I think. Other people might disagree. One cannot arbitrate for everybody's taste. One can only make suggestions, and I now regret having put some white thyme into my red and purple bed.

Another mistake was not to make up the soil thoroughly in the first instance. It ought to have had a lot of grit incorporated for drainage. After all, if you think of where thyme grows wild, on the Downs for instance, the drainage is pretty sharp. And, so far as is possible, one should try to reproduce the conditions that plants enjoy.

———————◆———————

Glorious roses: the hybrid musk 'Felicia' and hybrid perpetual 'Gloire de Ducher'.

For nine years the two little thyme lawns have given me much pleasure. Nine years is a long time to leave any plant growing in the same place: it exhausts its soil and needs renewing. They have not given much trouble. They never needed mowing, and they needed weeding only about four times a year. Now the time has come to dig them up and renew their soil to freshen them up when I hope they will go on for another nine years.

How generous they are in their growth! You dig up one clump and divide it into ten or twenty rooted plants, which you can dibble in six inches apart and make as huge a bed as you wish, with lots left over to plant among paving stones as an overspill.

HORIZONTAL CLIMBERS

An unusual way of treating clematis is to grow it horizontally instead of vertically. For this, you need a kind of oblong trellis of bamboo sticks, supported at each of the four corners on a stout little post, about two feet high from the ground; or a rectangle of rabbit wire or sheep wire will do equally well, besides probably proving more durable. The effect to be aimed at is a low, flat, open-work table top, under which you plant your plant, and allow it to grow up through. Every few days in the growing season, you will have to go round and weave the new strands in and out of the wire or trellis, for clematis grows at an amazing rate once it starts, and its instinct is to grow perpendicularly, not flatly; but do this as gingerly as you can, for clematis seems to resent the touch of the human hand.

Does all this sound too complicated? It isn't really, and the reward is great. For one thing, you will be able to gaze right down into the upturned face of the flower instead of having to crane your neck to observe the tangle of colour hanging perhaps ten or twenty feet above your head. The full beauty of the flower is thus exposed to you, in a way that it never is when you see it only from underneath. And for another thing, the clematis

Rosa 'Zephirine Drouhin'

itself will get the benefit of
shade on its roots, in this
case its own shade, with its
head in the sun, which is
what all clematis enjoy.

The big-flowered *jackmanii* type is the most
suitable for growing like this, or the Patens
group, because both these kinds have flat
flowers. The well-known dark purple *jackmanii*
looks spendid, or its variety 'Rubra'. 'Nelly
Moser' is a pale mauve, with a pink stripe; 'Gipsy Queen'
a very deep purple.

The same idea could be extended to many other climbers, say
honeysuckle, or the annual morning glory, and even to the
strong-growing kinds of rose. The hybrid perpetuals, such as
'Frau Karl Druschki', white, or 'Ulrich Brunner', cherry-red, or
'Hugh Dickson', dark red, or the old pink thornless rose, 'Zephirine Drouhin'
(hybrid bourbon) will break out from every joint if bent over in this way or merely
pegged down to the ground at the tip of the shoots. The extra crop of flowers you
will thus obtain imposes rather a strain on the plant, so leave only three or four
shoots and give a little encouragement with manure or compost.

OBLIGING ABUTILONS

A shrub which has given me great delight over at least four weeks of flowering
is *Abutilon vitifolium*, but before praising it let me list its drawbacks, always the more
prudent method. First, it is not a plant for harsh climates. Given a sheltered angle
between walls or hedges, it will survive a reasonable winter in the southern and, of
course, the south-western counties, but would not like being planted in the open in
some bleak spot of the Midlands or East Anglia. Second, it is not very long-lived, and
may die abruptly, leaving a painful blank. Third – no, there seems no third objection
to set against it, so now I can come on to the praise.

As its adjectival name suggests, it has a vine-like leaf, of a pale greenish-grey,
thickly clothed in May and June with five-petalled flowers either of pale lavender,
the colour of Parma violets, or a pure white with golden anthers. You must decide
for yourselves which you prefer, the mauve or the white. Having a predilection for
white flowers I gave my heart to the white, a ghostly apparition seen by moonlight.
The flowers are rather like a single hollyhock, which is comprehensible since the
abutilon belongs to the *Malvaceae* or mallows, but it also suggests a resemblance to
the tall Japanese anemone, if you can imagine a Japanese anemone deciding to turn
itself into a shrub.

It will grow ten feet high or more, quite quickly; and although it has this
unfortunate habit of suddenly dying, it can easily be kept going by its own seeds

which it produces in the usual squandering quantities Nature thinks necessary. A few seeds sown in a pot should supply enough young plants to replace their grandmothers. Seeds may come true, but one has to take the chance of getting the mauve or the white form, always rather an exciting experiment to see what one is going to get.

Abutilon vitifolium comes from Chile and was first introduced into Ireland in 1836, so it has been quite a long time in our gardens. A lovely cool-looking shrub for the spring months or early summer. I would recommend it every time. I think it ought to be well placed, against a dark background if possible, say a dark hedge to show up the pallor of the silvery leaf and the flower. A great deal depends on the right placing of any plant, as I always try to emphasise.

DRUNK ON ROSES

Drunk on roses, I look round and wonder which to recommend. Among the climbers, I do not believe that I have ever mentioned 'Lawrence Johnston', a splendid yellow, better than the very best butter, and so vigorous as to cover twelve feet of wall within two seasons. It does not seem to be nearly so well known as it ought to be, even under its old name 'Hidcote Yellow', although it dates back to 1923 and received an Award of Merit from the R.H.S. in 1948. The bud, of a beautifully pointed shape, opens into a loose, nearly-single flower which does not lose its colour up to the very moment when it drops. Eventually it will attain a height of thirty feet, but if you cannot afford the space for so rampant a grower, you have a sister seedling in 'Le Rêve', indistinguishable as to flower and leaf, but more restrained as to growth.

There is a fairly new hybrid musk, 'Grandmaster', which would associate well as a bush planted in front of either 'Lawrence Johnston' or 'Le Rêve'. This is an exquisite thing, a great improvement on the other hybrid musk, 'Buff Beauty', though that in all conscience

Rosa 'Grandmaster'

is lovely enough. 'Grandmaster' is nearly single, salmon-coloured on the outside and a very pale gold within, scentless, alas, which one does not expect of a musk, but that fault must be overlooked for the extreme beauty of the bush spattered all over as it were with large golden butterflies. These shrubby roses are invaluable, giving so little trouble and filling so wide an area at so little cost.

If the yellows are not to your liking, you have a perfect rose-pink in *Rosa gallica complicata*. Enormous single flowers borne all the length of the very long sprays. I cannot think why it should be called *complicata*, for it has a simplicity and purity of line which might come straight out of a Chinese drawing. This is a real treasure, if you can give it room to toss itself about as it likes; and whether you lightly stake it upright or allow it to trail must depend upon how you feel about it. Personally I think that its graceful untidiness is part of its charm, but whatever you do with it you can depend upon it to fill any corner with its renewed surprise in June.

A COURTYARD OF COLUMBINES

Not nearly enough use is made of that airy flower the columbine. Even the old *Aquilegia vulgaris* has its charm, and I confess that I never have the heart to tear it out from wherever it has chosen to sow itself, though I know that it is little more than a weed and is a nuisance in that it hybridises to the detriment of the choicer kinds. In fact, there are few flowers better disposed to hybridise amongst themselves, or, as one nurseryman puts it, "their morals leave much to be desired". In the case of the columbines, however, this is part of their attraction, for it means you may get chance seedlings of a colour you never anticipated.

Let me list their other advantages. They are perennial, which saves a lot of bother. They are hardy. They are light and graceful in a mixed bunch. They will put up with a certain amount of shade. They are easily grown from seed, and may be had in a surprising range of height and hue, from the tiny blue *alpina* whose inch of stature makes it suitable for rockeries, to the three-foot long-spurred hybrids in yellow, white, blue, mauve, pink, crimson-and-gold; and even, if you want something really out of the way, in green-and-brown. This last one is called 'Viridiflora', and is about a foot high. I regret that I do not know where to obtain its seed; a plant should be a good investment, as it will set seed of its own accord for future increase.

For any lucky person with the space to spare, I could imagine a small enclosed garden or, say, a three-sided courtyard such as you often find in old farmhouses. If the courtyard happened to be paved with flagstones, so much the better, for, as I never tire of saying, plants love to get between the cracks and send their roots down into the cool reaches of the soil beneath, thus preserving themselves from the minor enemy of frost and from the major enemy of damp. It is just such a little walled garden or courtyard that I envisage, blowing with a coloration of columbines.

JULY

This little space which scented box encloses
Is blue with lupins and is sharp with thyme.
My garden all is overblown with roses,
My spirit all is overblown with rhyme,
As like a drunked honeybee I waver
From house to garden and again to house,
And, undetermined which delight to favour,
On verse and rose alternately carouse.

Sonnet

A COOL, WHITE GARDEN

Provided one does not run the idea to death, and provided one has enough room, it is interesting to make a one-colour garden. It is something more than merely interesting. It is great fun and endlessly amusing as an experiment, capable of perennial improvement, as you take away the things that don't fit in, or that don't satisfy you, and replace them by something you like better.

There are two small internal gardens of this sort within my own garden. One of them is a typical cottage garden, a muddle of flowers, but all of them in the range of colour you might find in a sunset. I used to call it the sunset garden in my own mind before I even started to plant it up. I will not write about this now, for the sunset colours seem too hot in this month of July. I will write, rather, about the grey, green, white, silver garden which looks so cool on a summer evening.

I should like to use the old word *garth* for it, meaning a small piece of enclosed ground, usually beside a house or other building, for it is entirely enclosed, on one side by a high yew hedge and on the other sides by pink brick walls and a little Tudor house. It is divided into square beds by paths edged with lavender and box. But, as it is difficult to convey any impression of a place without the help of photographs, it would be wiser to confine myself to a list of the plants used to produce the cool, almost glaucous, effect we have aimed at.

There is an underplanting of various artemisias, including the old aromatic Southernwood; the silvery *Cineraria maritima*; the grey santolina or cotton lavender; and the creeping *Achillea ageratifolia*. Dozens of the white Regale lily (grown from seed) come up through these. There are white delphiniums of the Pacific strain; white eremurus; white foxgloves in a shady place on the north side of a wall; the

The White Garden seen from the tower showing the canopy of *Rosa longicuspes*.

foam of gypsophila; the white shrubby *Hydrangea paniculata* 'Grandiflora'; white cistus; white tree paeonies; *Buddleia nivea*; white campanulas and the white form of *Platycodon grandiflorum mariesii*, the Chinese balloon flower. There is a group of the giant Arabian thistle, pure silver, eight feet high. Two little sea buckthorns, and the grey willow-leaved *Pyrus salicifolia* sheltering the grey leaden statue of a Vestal Virgin. Down the central path goes an avenue of white climbing roses, straggling up old almond trees. Later on there will be white Japanese anemones and some white dahlias; but I do not like to think of later on. It is bad enough to have turned over into July, with the freshness of another May and June gone for ever.

SUMMER MULLEINS

Most of the verbascums (mulleins) are useful in the summer garden. The Cotswold hybrids are by now well known, 'Cotswold Beauty', 'Cotswold Queen', 'Cotswold Gem', and other members of their family, variously named but all looking as though clouds of small tawny or blushing moths had alighted all the way up the stalk, to remain poised there during the month of June. These hybrids are perennials, and moreover will sow themselves generously, so that once you have got them into your garden you need never be without them. Their only disadvantage, so far as I can see, is that they sometimes attract their own favourite brand of caterpillar, which eats the leaves into a semblance of lace-work; but he is very easily controlled, poor thing, by a dusting of derris powder.

The verbascum which has excited me this summer, however, is not one of the Cotswold range, but something quite new to me in my ignorance, called *Verbascum* 'Broussa'. Huge grey-green leaves, heavily dusted with flour, throwing up a spike six to seven feet tall, even more grey and woolly than the leaves. It fascinated me to watch this spike growing so rapidly, and to observe its pentagonal buds exploding one by one into the yellow flowers. They came gradually: a woolly grey bud one day, with a blunt yellow nose in the middle of it, and a flat yellow flower the next. They went on flowering for at least two months, through June and July.

I had planted my *Verbascum* 'Broussa' against the dark background of a yew hedge. They looked very handsome there; they looked like Roman candles, fireworks, tethered to the ground, but they also had the art of arranging themselves into grand curves, sweeping upwards, so that there was no upright monotony about them, nor did they demand any staking. It is a perennial and I fancy that it will ripen its own seed so that one should be able to harvest one's own supply for increase.

Near them I had a group of *Onopordum arabicum*, grown from seed. It was too young this summer to throw up its noble spike of blue thistle-like flowers, but its large grey leaves looked fine, with the same architectural quality as the leaves of acanthus, and the background of the yew hedge should be ideal for them.

THROUGH TINTED SPECTACLES

The other day I encountered a gentleman wearing amber-coloured spectacles. He was kind enough to say that I had a well-chosen range of colour in my garden. I expressed some surprise at this, since it was obvious that he could not be seeing any colours in their true colour, but must be seeing them in some fantastic alteration of tincture. "Yes," he said, "of course I do; it amuses me; try my glasses on," he said; "look at your roses; look also at your brown-tiled roofs; look at the clouds in the sky. Look," he said, handing them to me. I looked, and was instantly transferred into a different world. A volcanic eruption, or possibly an earthquake, seemed imminent. Alarming, perhaps, but how strange, how magical.

Everything had become intensified. All the greens of turf or trees had deepened. All the blues were cut out, or turned to a blackish-brown. The whites turned to a rich buttercup-yellow. The most extraordinary effect of all was when you switched over to the pink variations of colour. There has been some correspondence in the Press recently about that old favourite rose, 'Zephirine Drouhin'. Dear though she was to me, perfect in scent, vigorous in growth, magnificent in floraison (a lovely and expressive word we might well import from French into English, since we seem to have no equivalent in our language), and so kindly and obliging in having no thorns, never a cross word or a scratch as one picked her – dear though she was, I say, I had always deplored the crude pink of her complexion. It was her only fault. Seen through the magic glasses, she turned into a copper-orange; burnished, incredible.

'Zephirine Drouhin' has a romantic history, worthy of her breeze-like name. She derives from a hybrid found growing in 1817 in a hedge of roses in the Ile de Bour-bon, now called Réunion, off the east coast of Africa. This hybrid became the parent of the whole race of bour-bon roses, which in their turn have given rise to the modern roses we call hybrid perpetuals and hybrid teas. This is putting it very briefly, and seems to bear no relation to the great pink bush

Hydrangea paniculata
'Grandiflora'

Rosa 'Madame Plantier'

flowering in the summer garden under the name 'Zephirine Drouhin'. Who was Zephirine? Who was M. Drouhin? These are questions I cannot answer. They sound like characters in a novel by Flaubert. I know only that this gentle, thornless, full-bosomed rose turned into a fabulous flaming bush under the sorcery of tinted glasses.

PALE CLIMBERS

I am astonished and even alarmed by the growth which certain roses will make in the course of a few years. There is one called 'Madame Plantier', which we planted at the foot of a worthless old apple tree, vaguely hoping that it might cover a few feet of the trunk. Now it is 15 feet high with a girth of 15 yards, tapering towards the top like the waist of a Victorian beauty and pouring down in a vast crinoline stitched all over with its white sweet-scented clusters of flower.

'Madame Plantier' dates back, in fact, to 1835, just two years before Queen Victoria came to the throne, so she and the Queen may be said to have grown up together towards the crinolines of their maturity. Queen Victoria is dead, but 'Madame Plantier' still very much alive. I go out to look at her in the moonlight: she gleams, a pear-shaped ghost, contriving to look both matronly and virginal. She has to be tied up round her tree, in long strands, otherwise she would make only a big straggly bush; we have found that the best method is to fix a sort of tripod of bean-poles against the tree and tie the strands to that.

Another favourite white rose of mine is 'Paul's Lemon Pillar'. It should not be called white. A painter might see it as greenish, suffused with sulphur-yellow, and its great merit lies not only in the vigour of its growth and wealth of flowering, but also in the perfection of its form. The shapeliness of each bud has a sculptural quality which suggests curled shavings of marble. If one may imagine marble made of the softest ivory suède. The full-blown flower is scarcely less beautiful; and when the first explosion of bloom is over, a carpet of thick white petals covers the ground, so dense as to look as though it had been deliberately laid.

The old 'Madame Alfred Carrière' is likewise in full flower. Smaller than Paul's rose, and with no pretensions to a marmoreal shape, 'Madame Alfred', white, flushed with shell-pink, has the advantage of a sweet, true-rose scent, and will grow to the eaves of any reasonably proportioned house. I should like to see every Airey house in this country rendered invisible behind this curtain of white and green.

MOCK ORANGE BLOSSOM

I have been much struck this month by the beauty of the philadelphus. We used to call it syringa, with mock orange as its English name, but philadelphus seems to suit it nicely, meaning brotherly or sisterly love in Greek, suggesting a purity of love distinct from any sexual passion. Yet the thing is bridal. It makes huge bushes of the purest white. Brotherly or sisterly love may be all very well, but it is a truly nuptial thing, an epithalamium of a poem for young lovers.

I saw it foaming about in two famous gardens I recently went to in Gloucestershire. I saw it also in all the cottage gardens of that incomparable Cotswold country. It was everywhere; all over the place. I scolded myself for not having planted philadelphus in masses when I first started to make my garden. Had I done so years ago, I should have had huge bushes by now, but it is never too late.

I have got the dear old *Philadelphus coronarius*, that sweet-scented bush that takes one straight back to one's childhood. Three hundred years ago, Gerard the herbalist wrote that he had cut some flowers of this old plant, and laid them in his chamber, but found them of so unacquainted a savour that he could not take rest until he had cast them out of his chamber. This can mean only that he found the scent too strong. What I hadn't realised was that some of the later flowering sorts were almost equally generous of their scent. Now I know better. The little *microphyllus* may not be very showy but smells delicious in its small white flowers. *Erectus* is also sweet-scented. 'Belle Etoile' isn't; or at any rate I can't detect any scent in it. Perhaps that is the fault of my nose; anyhow it is so magnificent a shrub that we all ought to grow it.

The philadelphus family is so complicated that it is difficult to distinguish between them. They hybridise so freely amongst themselves that scarcely anybody knows now which are species and which are hybrids. Do we have to worry about this? Should we not rather plant as many as we can secure, this autumn, in the anticipation of great white bushes a few years hence?

THE INCENSE PLANT

A plant which I find always arouses a good deal of interest in the summer here is *Humea elegans*. Visitors

Philadelphus coronarius 'Belle Etoile'

walk round sniffing and saying, "What is that curious smell of incense? One might imagine oneself in an Italian cathedral instead of an English garden". They are quite right, for its other name is the incense plant.

Eventually they track it down to a six to eight-foot-tall plant, with large, pointed dark green leaves, and a branching spike of feathery cedar wood-coloured flowers. It is neither showy nor conspicuous, and nothing but the scent would lead you to it among its more garish companions, such as the delphiniums; yet it is graceful in its growth and well deserves its adjective *elegans*. It makes its influence felt in more subtle ways than by a great splash of colour. It steals across the air as potently and pervasively as the sweetbriar on a damp evening. I stick it into odd corners, where people pass, or sit on benches, and pause for a moment before going on their way.

A native of Australia, it is not hardy here, and must be treated as a half-hardy annual, sown under glass in February or March, kept away from frost, and planted out in the late half of May or beginning of June. For this reason I cannot advise anyone to grow it who has not the advantage of a frost-proof greenhouse in which to raise it; but those fortunate gardeners who have even a tiny, warmed greenhouse might well experiment with a few seeds in a pot: six seeds will give six plants, and six plants will be enough to scent the garden, especially if planted under the windows. It likes a rich soil; it would love to be fed with liquid manure, and will grow all the better if you have time to give it this extra diet; but if you have not the time – and who has the time to attend to all these extra and special requirements? – it will do adequately well in ordinary garden soil, and will give you all the reward you can reasonably demand.

An additional attraction is that the flowering spike will last for at least six months indoors if you cut it off in autumn before the rain has come to sodden it. I kept some sprays of it in a vase for so long that I began to loathe the sight of the thing: it turned dusty long before it started to fade and die; it reminded me of those everlasting flowers, the helichrysums, which are only too everlasting indeed.

You can save and ripen your own seed of it by cutting a spray or two and lying it out on sheets of paper in a sunny place, and thus you need never be without it again once you have got it going in your garden. The supply of seed died out during the war, but is now obtainable from some of the big seedsmen.

I think I should add a word of warning. Some people appear to be allergic to *Humea elegans*, which brings them out in a rash which is anything but elegant. (Some primulas have this effect on some people.) It is a chancy danger which I would not wish any reader to incur.

M Y FAVOURITE ROSES

Sometimes someone asks me which are my favourites among the various old roses that I grow. This is really an impossible question to answer, since one changes

The weeping pear, white foxgloves and silver foliage plants in the White Garden.

Rosa alba 'Celestial'

one's mind from day to day. Each one, as it separately comes out, seems to eclipse its predecessor in charm or beauty, but on the whole I am not sure I would not plump for *Rosa alba* 'Celestial' and for 'Fantin Latour', which may be either a bourbon rose or a centifolia. Does it matter which, except to the experts who so far never seem to reach agreement?

How can I describe *alba* 'Celestial'? I am holding up a sprig of it in my left hand as I try to write about it with my right. I look very closely; I peer. I see the pale pink petals; I see the golden boss. I see the pointed buds not yet unfolded and whose life-fulfilment I have destroyed by picking them before they had a chance to come out. Yet all this close observation cannot convey any impression at all of what *alba* 'Celestial' looks like grown in the open as a shrub rose, when those pale shell-pink flowers combine in a self-ordained way with the blue-green foliage. It has to be seen as a shrub, to be appreciated at its best.

'Fantin Latour' may have been painted by Fantin Latour himself, or it may have been named in his honour. Here, again, I cannot see that it much matters, so long as we can get this lovely thing in our gardens, as we still can. It does not grow too large and is of manageable size for a small garden. Its colouring of a delicate pale pink is easy to place anywhere: it will not swear or quarrel with the other colours.

How silly it is, all the same, to pick out favourites amongst the wealth offered by the old shrub roses. I think of 'Cardinal de Richelieu', and 'Tour de Malakoff' and 'Roi des Pourpres' and many others, and wonder in bewilderment which I like best. And then I think of the hybrid musks, lovely 'Penelope' who scents my garden and my room, cut in sheaves from a hedge planted along a fence only two years ago. If anybody wants a rose hedge, I would advise 'Penelope'. But if anybody wants a really exquisite shrub rose, I would advise *alba* 'Celestial' or 'Fantin Latour'.

SEE-THROUGH FLOWERS

Flowers vary in their value, not only in their form and colour but also in their consistency. Some, like the phlox or the stock, are monuments of solidity; others, like the gypsophila, clouds of lightness and transparency. These are the see-through flowers.

Gypsophila is perhaps the first that comes to the mind, a true foam which should never have been allowed to catch sight of a sweet pea. 'Bristol Fairy' is the best, and there is also a pale pink variety, 'Flamingo', less often seen. But when you come to think of it, many other plants share the lacy quality of gypsophila. Heuchera, for example, either pink or red, and *Heucherella* 'Bridget Bloom' both add a touch of airy frivolity to the front of the border. So does *Heuchera* 'Major', rather taller, coming on usefully in the middle distance.

Far taller again, *Macleaya cordata*, the plume poppy, is for the back of the border; its usual colour is a strawy buff, but a pink version obtainable under the name 'Coral Plume' is much to be recommended, particularly if it can be grown where it will catch the rays of the afternoon sun. Even the humble little London pride is not to be despised as an edging, especially if you get the kind called *Saxifraga umbrosa primuloides* 'Elliott's Variety'.

Thalictrum is a true see-through flower. There used to be an unforgetable double border, with a broad grass path down the middle, at Hurstmonceux Castle in Sussex, composed of delphiniums and thalictrum, alternating in their massive blue and their thin delicate purple, as happy a marriage as ever I did see. I think there was lavender all along the front, its purple spikes like thousands of little lances forming almost a see-through hedge on it own account; one saw the two borders in perspective from the castle, which is the way that all borders ought to be seen.

Some of the brooms might almost qualify, so light and graceful are they. The creamy 'Moonlight', the pale yellow *Cytisus praecox*, and the golden rain of the Etna broom, *Genista aetnensis*, if not exactly see-through plants, come very close with their myriad butterfly-like petals. And, amongst other shrubs, what about the wig-plant or smoke plant, *Cotinus coggygria*, smothered under its spidery heads of inflorescence?

Rosa 'Fantin Latour'

For those who do not mind the introduction of a semi-weed into their garden, there is a pink form of pimpinella, the familiar Queen Anne's lace, of our road-verges where no iniquitous weed-killer has been sprayed. I know that some people are turning part of their garden into a wild or natural garden: here is the ideal plant for them, for it would not matter how much it spread. *P. major rosea* is its name, and it is of some interest that its Greek relation, *P. anisum,* should be nothing less than our old friend aniseed.

The giant *Crambe cordifolia* from the Caucasus may tower into a flower-head seven feet tall, very lacy against a dark hedge or blue sky. Its little cousin, *C. maritima*, a British native, is just merely sea kale.

*T*REE POPPIES

A beautiful thing in flower just now is the Californian tree poppy. It is not exactly a shrub, and not exactly a herbaceous plant; you can call it a sub-shrub if you like; whatever you call it will make no difference to its beauty. With grey-green glaucous leaves, it produces its wide, loose white-and-gold flowers on slender stems five or six feet in height. The petals are like crumpled tissue paper; the anthers quiver in a golden swarm at the centre. It is very lovely and delicate.

I don't mean delicate as to its constitution, except perhaps in very bleak districts. Once you get it established it will run about all over the place, being what is known as a root-runner, and may even come up in such unlikely and undesirable positions as the middle of a path. I know one which has wriggled its way under a brick wall and come up manfully on the other side. The initial difficulty is to get it established, because it hates being disturbed and transplanted, and the best way to cheat it of this reluctance is to grow it from root cuttings in pots. This will entail begging a root cutting from a

Romneya coulteri

friend or an obliging nurseryman. You can then tip it out of its pot into a complaisant hole in the place where you want it to grow, and hope that it will not notice what has happend to it. Plants, poor innocents, are easily deceived.

The Latin name of the tree poppy is *Romneya*. There are two named sorts, *Romneya coulteri* and *Romneya trichocalyx*. They are both much the same, except for a few botanical differences. *R. coulteri* is perhaps the better. It likes a sunny place and not too rich a soil. It will get cut down in winter most likely, but this does not matter, because it will spring up again, and in any case it does not appear to flower on the old wood, so the previous season's growth is no loss. In fact, you will probably find it advisable to cut it down yourself in the spring, if the winter frosts have not already done it for you.

HARDY HOHERIA

A good companion to the tree poppy is a tall, twelve-foot shrub called *Hoheria lyallii*. I can't think why people don't grow it more often, if they have a sheltered corner and want a tall shrub that flowers in that awkward time between late June and early July, smothered in white-and-gold flowers of the mallow family, and sows itself in such profusion that you could have a whole forest of it if you had the leisure to prick out the seedlings and the space to replant them.

It really is a lovely thing, astonishing me every year with its profusion. I forgot about it; and then there it is again with its flowers coming in their masses suggesting philadelphus, for which it might easily be mistaken, but even more comely than any philadelphus, I think, thanks to the far prettier and paler leaf. A native of the South Island of New Zealand, it has the reputation of not being quite hardy in the colder parts of this country. That is why I said grow it in a sheltered corner. All I can tell you is that it has survived many frosty winters here in Kent (not so favourable a climate as, say, Sussex, let alone the farther western counties), including the dreadful ice-rain winter of 1946-47 and the cruel February of 1956, and that seems a good enough recommendation or character reference for giving so lovely a thing a chance.

It has other advantages. It doesn't dislike a limy soil, always important for people who garden on chalk and can't grow rhododendrons or azaleas or kalmias or any of the ericaceous plants. It doesn't like rich feeding, which tends to make it produce leaf rather than flower. This means an economy in compost or organic manure or inorganic fertilisers which could be better expended elsewhere. Bees love it. It is busy with bees, making their midsummer noise as you pass by. When I first knew and grew it, it called itself *Plagianthus lyalli*. Now it prefers to call itself *Hoheria*. Let it, for all I care. So far as I am concerned, it is the thing to grow behind the tree poppy, which it will out-top and will complement with the same colouring of the pale green leaves and the smaller white flowers, in a candid white and green and gold bridal effect more suitable, one would think, to April than to July.

DEAD-HEADING THE ROSES

Dead-heading the roses on a summer evening is an occupation to carry us back into a calmer age and a different century. Queen Victoria might still be on the throne. All is quiet in the garden; the paths are pale; our silent satellite steals up the sky; even the aeroplanes have gone to roost and our own nerves have ceased to twangle. There is no sound except the hoot of an owl, and the rhythmic snip-snip of our own secateurs, cutting the dead heads off, back to a new bud, to provoke new growth for the immediate future.

A pleasurable occupation for us, when we have the time to spare; it must be even more pleasurable to the roses. They get relieved of those heavy rain-sodden lumps of spent flowers which are no good to themselves or to anyone else. There is something satisfying in the extreme, in the thought that we are doing good both to our rose bushes and to ourselves in our snip-snip back towards the young shoot longing to develop, and something most gratifying in watching the pale green shoot lengthening inch by inch in a surprisingly short time.

The shrubby roses have lasted longer than usual this year, presumably because no hot days have burnt them up, but they are rapidly going over and their short season is a thing of the past. I notice that the alba rose known as 'Great Maiden's Blush' holds her flowers longer than most. This is a very beautiful old rose, many-petalled, of an exquisite shell-pink clustering among the grey-green foliage, extremely sweet-scented, and for every reason perfect for filling a squat bowl indoors. In the garden she is not squat at all, growing six to seven feet high and wide in proportion, thus demanding a good deal of room, perhaps too much in a small border but lovely and reliable to fill a stray corner.

All the old roses have a touch of romance about them: the 'Great Maiden's Blush' has more than a touch of romance in her various names alone. She has also been called 'La Séduisante', and 'Cuisse de Nymphe' or the 'Nymph's Thigh'. When she blushed a particularly deep pink, she was called 'Cuisse de Nymphe émue'. I will not insult the French language by attempting to translate this highly expressive name. I would suggest only that Cyrano de Bergerac would have appreciated the implication, and that any young couple with an immature garden and an even more immature pram-age daughter might well plant the 'Great Maiden', alias 'La Séduisante'.

*T*IME FOR ALSTROEMERIAS

There are some moments when I feel pleased with my garden, and other moments when I despair. The pleased moments usually happen in spring, and last up to the middle of June. By that time all the freshness has gone off; everything has become heavy; everything has lost that adolescent look, that look of astonishment at its own youth. The middle-aged spread has begun.

It is then that the alstroemerias come into their own. They are in flower now, so this is the opportunity to go and see them, either in a local nurseryman's plot, or in a private garden, or at a flower show. The yellow Peruvian lily, *A. aurantiaca*, was and is a common sight in cottage gardens and old herbaceous borders, where it was regarded almost as a weed, but it has been superseded by the far more beautiful Ligtu hybrids, in varied colours of coral and buff, and by *A. haemantha*, a brilliant orange. (Keep the orange away from the coral, for they do not mix well together, and whoever it was who said Nature made no mistakes in colour harmony was either colour-blind or a sentimentalist. Nature makes the most hideous mistakes; and it is up to us gardeners to control and correct them.)

May I insist on two or three points for growing them, dictated to me by practical experience? First, grow them from seed, sown on the spot where you wish them to continue their existence. This is because the roots are extremely brittle, and they loathe being transplanted. So suspicious are they of transplantation that even seedlings carefully tipped out of pots seem to sense that something precarious and unsettling is happening to them, and resent it in the unanswerable way of plants by the simple protest of death. Second, sow them either when the seed is freshly harvested, or, better still, in early spring. Third, sow them in a sunny, well-drained place. Fourth, the seedlings would like a little protection in winter if there is a hard frost. Some bracken will do, scattered over them. Once established, they are hardy enough to withstand anything but a particularly bad winter. It is only the young that are tender, needing a little love and care. After observing all these instructions you will not have to worry about them any more, beyond staking them with twiggy sticks as soon as they reappear every year six inches above the ground, for the stems are fragile and easily broken: they flop and snap and lose their beauty, lying flat after a thunderstorm of rain or a sudden gale, such as we get from time to time in our usually temperate country. This is a counsel of caution. Prop up your alstroemerias, if you take my advice to grow them, by twiggy pea-sticks.

They are the perfect flower for cutting, lasting weeks in water in the house. Outdoors, you will find that the clumps increase in size and beauty, with self-sown seedlings coming up all over the near neighbourhood.

Alstroemeria ligtu hybrids

And August duly brought
Swarms of a summer enemy, of those
Small samurai in lacquered velvet dressed,
Innumerable in their vermin breed
As fierce and fiery as a spark of gleed,
Scavengers on a gormandising quest
To batten on the treasure of our crops
Of promised fruit, our gages, Golden Drops,
Our peaches downy as a youthful cheek,
Our nectarines, in adolescence sleek;
They came, destructive though we sought their nest,
Those fiends that rustic oracles call wopse.

The Garden

A GOLDEN GROUP
One of the nicest things about gardening is the sudden surprise we may get when something that we arranged years ago comes into its own and at last starts doing what we had intended it to do. We must admit that dusk is probably the kindest hour, lengthening the shadows, intensifying the colours, and obliterating the weeds, but nevertheless I was not disappointed in the glare of the following morning by the great golden group I had observed in the afterglow of a lingering sunset.

It was a group composed of ordinary, easy things, and it was simply their collusion in flowering all together at the same time that made them so effective. In the foreground was a rounded shrub of cinquefoil, *Potentilla fruticosa*, with silvery leaves spattered by lemon-yellow flowers. Behind this arose the taller, flat-headed yellow yarrow, *Achillea filipendulina*, and then behind that the feathery meadow-rue, *Thalictrum flavum glaucum*, a fluffy, saffron version of the brush we used to push up lamp-glasses before we had electric light. A few pale evening primroses had poked their untidy way upwards through a huge bush of the truly aureate St. John's Wort, *Hypericum patulum* 'Forrestii', already massing the varnished buttercup of its half-crown-sized flower, and many buds coming on in promise. All this was good enough, but towering above the lot came the dripping glory of a great Mount Etna broom, *Genista aetnensis*, ten feet high, an arrested fountain of molten gold.

Now, all these are easy going plants, within the scope of every purse and experience or lack of experience, and if anybody had the space requisite to repeat this grouping in some lost corner where the sunset strikes, I think he would be pleased. Since one is never satisfied, however, I started making mental notes for

A view of the Cottage Garden from the tower, with the climbing rose
'Alchemist' in the foreground.

improvement. The 'Hidcote' variety of the St. John's Wort, for instance, is a finer thing than the type introduced by Forrest from China. Why hadn't I planted the 'Hidcote'hypericum in the first instance? One should always plant the best, but one is ignorant to start with, and it takes years of floundering before one learns. And why had I not sent up some rockets of the giant mullein, *Verbascum olympicum*, to match the suspended fireworks of the Mount Etna broom? Why, indeed? I hope next year to repair my half-misspent time.

*B*IRTH OF THE BOURBONS
If you were born with a romantic nature, all roses must be crammed with romance, and if a particular rose originated on an island the romance must be doubled, for an island is romantic in itself.

The island I refer to lies off the southeast coast of Africa, near Mauritius. It used to be called the Ile Bourbon, now called Réunion. The inhabitants of this small island had the pleasing habit of using roses for their hedges: only two kinds, the Damask rose and the China rose. These two married in secret; and one day, in 1817, the curator of the botanic garden on the Ile Bourbon noticed a seedling which he transplanted and grew on, a solitary little bastard which has fathered or mothered the whole race we now call the bourbon roses.

It is curious to find Mr Edward Bunyard writing in 1936 in his book *Old Garden Roses* that the bourbon roses "are now almost forgotten", and listing only four as being "still obtainable" ('Hermosa', 'Bourbon Queen', 'Louise Odier', and 'Mme Pierre Oger'). He does not even mention 'Zéphirine Drouhin', the rose which so far back as 1868 decided to discard armaments and has been known as

Hypericum 'Hidcote'

the thornless rose ever since. This shows how taste has changed within the last twenty years, for it is now possible to obtain at least two dozen different varieties.

Far from being forgotten, now that the shrub roses have returned to favour, the bourbon roses include some of the most desirable. Their scent alone makes one realise the extent to which they have inherited that quality from their damask parent; one has only to think of 'Mme Isaac Pereire' and 'Mme Pierre Oger', admittedly two of the most fragrant roses in cultivation. We all have our scented favourites; and someone is bound to say, "What about 'Parfum de l'Hay'?", but I must still support the claims of these two ladies in the bourbon group.

The cross has resulted in an oddly varied lot. There is 'Coupe de Hebe', 1840, which you might easily mistake for a centifolia or cabbage rose; and if you like the striped roses there are 'Honorine de Brabant' and 'Commandant Beaurepaire', 1874, pink and white like 'Rosa Mundi', but not, I contend, as good as that ancient 'Rose of the World'. Among the more recent crosses, 'Zigeuner Knabe', 1909, makes the most swagger-boastful bush you could set at any corner; a reddish purple, it looks more like a Cardinal fully robed, about to set off in procession, than like the 'Gypsy Boy' we call it in English.

CHINESE BELL FLOWERS

An effective splash of truly imperial purple may be had in the July-August border with a group of the Chinese bell flower, *Platycodon grandiflorum*. It may be raised from seed sown in spring, though, being a herbaceous perennial, it cannot be expected to flower during the first summer of its life. True, a first-season flowering is claimed for a variety called praecox, but I cannot speak of it from experience.

The bell flower, or balloon flower as it is sometimes called, resembles a campanula of a singularly rich colour, and does, in fact, belong to the same botanical family. Its shape charms me, when it first appears as a five-sided bud like a tiny lantern, so tightly closed as though its little seams had been stitched together, with the further charm that you can pop it like a fuchsia, if you are so childishly minded. This, I need hardly, say, is not good for the eventual flower. Left to its natural development, it expands into a five-petalled bell of deep violet, so beautifully veined that it is worth holding a single bloom up to the light, for it is one of those blooms which repay a close examination, revealing not only the delicate veining but also the pale stamens grouped round the sapphire-blue of the pistil.

Such examination may be a private pleasure, and is unlikely to be the principal reason for which we grow this sumptuous alien from China and Manchuria. It is for the splash in the border that it will be chiefly esteemed, a value scarcely to be exaggerated. I should like to see it associated with the feathery spires of *Thalictrum dipterocarpum*, a meadow rue, especially the variety called 'Hewitt's Double', the maidenhair-fern-like foliage and the cloud of innumerable small mauve flowers of the thalictrum coming up through the greater solidity of the purple bell-flower; but alas, the thalictrum will have nothing to say to me, patiently though I may plant and replant it, so I must content myself with recommending the idea to other, more fortunate, people.

The bell flower, at any rate, presents no difficulty and seems completely happy in ordinary soil in the sun, near the front of the border for it grows no taller than eighteen inches to two feet. One can grow a matching pansy or viola in front of it.

MY SUNSET GARDEN

Mid-August means the beginning of autumn, so we had better bravely make up our minds to it. Not that I have anything to say against autumn, as such. On certain days we may well be tempted to think it the most richly beautiful of seasons. It is only as a portent that we deplore it.

In a small square garden enclosed by holly hedges, I have been making notes of some plants in flower just now. They are all in the same range of colour – yellow, red, and orange – which explains why people often call it the sunset garden. At its best, it glows and flames. The dark hedges enhance the effect. Ideally, the hedges ought to be draped in ropes and curtains of the scarlet *Tropaeolum speciosum*, the flame creeper so rampant in the North; but this must be a Scottish Nationalist by conviction, for it will have little to say to Sassenach persuasions.

The rest of the little garden makes up for the lack. There are red hot pokers, tiger lilies, montbretias, and that thing which looks like a giant montbretia, antholyza, inevitably known as Aunt Eliza though nobody's Aunt Eliza could ever have looked so garish. The yellows are represented by the shrubby St. John's Wort, *Hypericum patulum* 'Hidcote'; I know the 'Rowallane' hypericum is better, but it isn't as hardy, and there doesn't seem much to choose between them. More yellows come in that coarse, tall, feathery groundsel, *Senecio tanguticus*, and in some gaillardias and in some belated yarrows and potentillas, with golden pansies as a groundwork in front of some 'Orange Bedder' snapdragons. Some *Lilium henryi*, one of the easiest of lilies, rise taller than a tall man amongst rose bushes of 'Mrs Van Rossem'; a patch of zinnias gives a dash of orange just where it is needed; the dahlia 'Bishop of Llandaff' sets its dark-green leaves and dark-red flower in a shady corner; the brilliance of the new hybrid, *Venidio-arctotis*, blazes in a narrow bed just where the sun strikes to make it open.

Have I exaggerated? Of course I have. The little garden was not quite like that, but it came very close to the idea, and there seems no reason why one day it should not fulfil the conception of its owner. That is the whole essence and excitement of gardening: to conceive a picture in the mind, and gradually year by year to improve it towards its completion.

INCREASING THE PINKS

The two most attractive ways, to my mind, of growing pinks and dianthus are in a dry wall and between grey paving stones. They also look charming and smell delicious grown in a long strip beside a garden path, but if a dry wall or a paved terrace are available, there, I would say, is the place for them.

I do not suppose many people bother much about the difference between a pink and a dianthus. Mr Will Ingwersen himself, a great authority on the family, says the precise differences are not easy to define, and adds "It is not sufficient to say that pinks are the hybrids as opposed to the natural species, for there are many hybrid dianthus which are not pinks". So perhaps we may leave it at that. Most of us, at any rate, flatter ourselves that we know a pink when we see one.

I write about them because this is the time to propagate them. Cuttings, taken from non-flowering shoots, with or without a heel, will root easily if set in a pot of sharp silver sand mixed with a very little finely sieved peat. Five parts sand to one part peat is about the proportion. Mr Ingwersen recommends putting the pots into a closed frame for a start but I am sure we all have gardening friends who simply shove their cuttings into a V-shaped trench in the open ground, made with the oblique cut of a spade and filled with sharp sand along the bottom, tread firmly, and hope for the best. And the best usually happens. Not 100 per cent perhaps, but surely 75 per cent, which should be enough to satisfy anybody.

There are also pipings. A piping is a young shoot which can be slid out of its stem by hand, and used in the same way as a cutting, but as these are more likely to be found in spring we need not bother about them now.

Then there is layering. This is a very easy method with the strong, tough varieties. You simply take a long, strong shoot, make a slit in it with a sharp knife, and peg it down into a prepared heap of sand. Old-fashioned hairpins, stout as miniature pitch-forks, are useful for the pegging-down, and I imagine they can still be bought, or filched from an aunt approaching her hundredth birthday.

So much for propagation. Now as to soil. The dwellers on an alkaline or limy soil will be in heaven when it comes to growing pinks. Yet the dwellers on neutral soil need not despair. So long as the dianthus is given good drainage and full sunshine we can depend on it to give a most generous return.

Oh, rabbits. They love all forms of pinks, especially young plants and cuttings. I know I have said this before but there can be no harm in repeating it. If your young plants get nibbled, water them with Epsom salt. That keeps rabbits off, but you have to renew the application after a heavy shower of rain.

BACK TO THE BOURBONS

Among the bourbon roses, lack of space compelled me to omit 'Mme Lauriol de Barny', and indeed

Dianthus 'Gran's Favourite'

Rosa 'Blairi No 2'

she is very large and proud. (I am aware that the French do not recognise her as a true bourbon.)

At a distance, but for the foliage, you might mistake her for a small paeony. Dating back to 1868, she has all the rosy lavishness of ladies of the Second Empire. I wish I could find out who Mme Lauriol was in real life, to have so sumptuous a flower called after her. I suspect that she may have belonged to the *haute cocotterie* of Paris at that date, or possibly I misjudge her and she may have been the perfectly respectable wife of some M. Barny, perhaps a rose-grower at Lyon. Someone ought to write the biographies of persons who have had roses named in their honour. Who was Mme Hardy? Who was Charles de Mills? I don't know, and I long for a *Who's Who* to correct my ignorance.

'Souvenir de la Malmaison', 1843, is easier to place as to name, although Josephine de Beauharnais can never have seen it. I suppose there will be screams if I say that this famous rose has never been one of my favourites. A perfect bloom, yes; but how often do we get one? It all too easily goes brown and sodden. The best thing I have to say for it is that it played its part in producing 'Gloire de Dijon', that fragrant crumpled straw-coloured old stager, equally charming as a climber or as a bush. 'Variegata di Bologna' is a fairly recent production, 1909, and is said to be a strong grower on rich soils. It looks miserable in my garden, greatly to my regret, for I know of no other rose with its colouring: violet stripes on a white background. Mr Graham Thomas suggests that it might do well under a north-west wall, with a cool root-run. No doubt I have planted it in too sunny a place.

This does not by any means exhaust the list of the bourbon roses. I have omitted 'La Reine Victoria', who appeared in 1872, although I have mentioned her child, 'Mme Pierre Oger'. 'Mme Ernst Calvat' I have never seen, but know by repute as one of the best, pink and scented, and suitable for growing up a pillar. 'Roi des Pourpres', now renamed 'Prince Charles', is not to my mind amongst the best of the violet or lilac roses; for this colour I would rather go to 'Cardinal Richelieu', a gallica, or

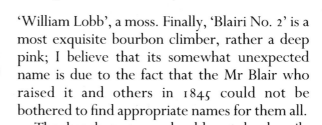

'William Lobb', a moss. Finally, 'Blairi No. 2' is a most exquisite bourbon climber, rather a deep pink; I believe that its somewhat unexpected name is due to the fact that the Mr Blair who raised it and others in 1845 could not be bothered to find appropriate names for them all.

The bourbon roses should not be heavily pruned, and indeed their full beauty can be displayed only when they are allowed to grow into the great tall bushes natural to them. Dead and twiggy wood should be cut out. How easy to say, and how scratchy to do.

MY MYRTLE

I have a myrtle growing on a wall. It is only the common myrtle, *Myrtus communis*, but I think you would have to travel far afield to find a lovelier shrub for July and August flowering. The small, pointed, dark-green leaves are smothered at this time of year by a mass of white flowers with quivering centres of the palest green-yellow, so delicate in their white and gold that it appears as though a cloud of butterflies had alighted on the dark shrub.

The myrtle is a plant full of romantic associations in mythology and poetry, the sacred emblem of Venus and of love, though why Milton called it brown I never could understand, unless he was referring to the fact that the leaves, which are by way of being evergreen, do turn brown in frosty weather or under a cold wind. Even if it gets cut down in winter there is nothing to worry about, for it springs up again, at any rate, in the south of England. In the north it might be grateful for a covering of ashes or fir-branches over the roots. It strikes very easily from cuttings, and a plant in a pot is a pretty thing to possess, especially if it can be stood near the house door, where the aromatic leaves may be pinched as you go in and out. In very mild counties, such as Cornwall, it should not require the protection of a wall, but may be grown as a bush or small tree in the open, or even, which I think should be most charming of all, into a small grove suggestive of Greece and her nymphs.

The flowers are followed by little inky berries, which in their turn are quite decorative, and would probably grow if you sowed a handful of them.

PALE BROOMS

It surprises me that people should not grow the brooms more freely in their gardens. We all know the wild broom, as golden yellow as the gorse, and far more graceful, less crabbed and rebarbative; but how many of us realise that there are other varieties of startling colours to enliven our gardens in April and May?

They are all desirable, and they should be especially valuable to people whose gardens are on a poor, hungry soil. They seem to enjoy being starved. Large lumps of manure have no attraction for them. Stones and gravel and as much sunshine as possible is what they like; but as they are most accommodating they will oblige you by growing almost anywhere within reason that you choose to set them. The only thing they appear to resent is being transplanted; so if you intend to follow my advice

and order some of them for planting this coming autumn, you must insist that your nurseryman delivers them from what he will technically call ex-pots. This means that they will scarcely notice their removal from one place of growth to another.

Another point I ought to mention is that the brooms are not very long-lived. After ten years or so they tend to die. Still, ten years is a reasonably good span of life for a plant.

The ones I want to write about now are the paler ones; the white ones, the virginal ones, the moonlit ones, the ones that look moonlit even when the sun is high. There is *Cytisus praecox*, a little shrub smothered in butterfly flowers in April, as pretty as a girl going to her first debutante dance. Then there is the broom rightly called 'Moonlight'; its name tells you what it is like, and suggests the nocturnal illumination which shows it up at its best. A full moon high in the heavens, gently diffusing its strange magical light, so different from the strong masculine light of the sun; a blending of moonlight with the white broom, a union of ghosts to be seen, not to be described. It reminds me of the old music-hall song, forgotten now:

Who were you with last night, last night,
Who was that peachy, creamy, dreamy
Vision of pure delight?

The old song brings nostalgic memories, brought by the white broom called 'Moonlight' vividly to mind.

The brooms have many other romantic associations, going right back into the early centuries of our English history and our kings. The name Plantagenet derives from *Planta genista*, the Latin for one group of the brooms, because a Count of Anjou, pilgrim to the Holy Land, adopted a sprig

Cytisus praecox 'Alba'

of broom as his crest and symbol. It was then thought to be a symbol of humility, but by the time Shakespeare came to handle it a royal dignity had attached itself to the humble broom:

Famous Plantagenet, most gracious Prince . . .

The moment one touches Shakespeare, one begins to marvel at how much he exactly knew. When, for instance, he wrote in Henry VI:

I'll plant Plantagenet: root him up who dares. . . .

did he know, as any gardener would know, that the brooms, *Planta genista*, will not endure being dug up? Root him up who dares.

Practical moral: insist on your nurseryman giving you your brooms in pots.

TIPS FOR LILIES

A lot of people have a lot of trouble with lilies. I have myself. I try. I fail. I despair. Then I try again. Only last week did it occur to me to go and ask for advice from a famous grower of lilies in my neighbourhood, which was the obvious and sensible thing to do. I might have thought of it before. Surely he will not mind my passing on the hints he gave me, especially if it leads to an encouragement to grow some varieties of this supremely beautiful family.

There are four cardinal points, he said, like the compass. Point 1: good drainage is essential; no stagnant moisture, even if it means digging out a hole and putting a layer of crocks or coarse clinker at the bottom. Point 2: make up a suitable bed to receive your bulbs, a bed rich in humus, which means leaf mould, peat, compost, chopped bracken, or whatever form of humus you can command. Point 3: never plant lily

bulbs which have been out of the ground too long or have had their basal roots cut off. Reject these, even if you find them offered at cheap rates in the horiticultural department of some chain stores. Lily bulbs should be lifted fresh and replanted quickly, with their basal roots intact; therefore it is advisable to obtain them from any reputable nurseryman, who will pack them in moist peat and will never allow them to dry out before despatch. Point 4: divide when they become overcrowded.

Finally, he said, remember that nothing makes a finer mulch than bracken cut green, chopped up into short pieces, and allowed to rot. He deprecated the use of lawn-grass mowings; of artificial fertilisers; and of over-fresh organic manure. Manure, he said, should never be allowed to come into contact with the bulb itself; it should be placed well beneath it, or used as a top mulch. Bone meal, he said, was always safe and useful.

To these hints I might add another. Most lilies dislike what professional gardeners call "movement of air", which in plain English means wind or a draught. I have also discovered by experience that the Regal lily, *Lilium regale*, likes growing amongst some covering shelter such as southernwood (old man) or one of the artemisias. I suppose because the foliage gives protection to the young lily-growth against late frosts, but also because some plants take kindly to one another in association. Certainly the long white trumpets of the lily look their majestic best emerging above the grey-green cloud of these fluffy, gentle, aromatic herbs.

*F*OR SOMBRE CORNERS

It sometimes happens that a secluded corner in a garden offers an opportunity for a self-contained planting-picture. It might be in the angle formed by the junction of two walls or two hedges; it might be within a bay amongst shrubs; it might be in a small yard; it might even be on either side of the door into a potting shed. The only essential is that it shall be somewhere apart, so that the shape and the colour scheme shall not become confused among other distractions to the eye. It must be, as it were, within its own frame.

Such a picture suggested itself to me almost accidentally. It would be original, if somewhat funereal, and I would not commend it except to the fastidious gardener. The sort of gardener who is not afraid of what some people would call gloom, for the plants involved are all on the mournful side. Sullen and sombre beauties, they have the dark richness of some fruits, certain plums for instance, and 'Black Hamburgh' grapes, and the inside of figs. At the back of my group I would put *Cotinus coggygria* 'Foliis Purpureis', the large-growing bush with plum-coloured foliage; and in the front of that I would put *Veratrum nigrum*, and then I would have the very ordinary herbaceous *Salvia nemorosa*, sometimes called *Salvia superba*, whose reddish bracts in August would look just right, and then in front I would have the strange fleshy *Sedum telephium* 'Atropurpureum'; and amongst them all I would cram bulbs of *Allium sphaerocephalum* by the dozen, for it flowers at the wanted time of year and is of the wanted colour; and finally to fill up any possible gap I would sow seeds in spring of the mountain orach, *Atriplex hortensis* 'Rubra', that decorative and much-neglected annual.

Of these six plants I have mentioned, only two are likely to be unfamiliar to the fastidious gardener, and perhaps not even to him. I mean the sedum and the veratrum. If he wants to obtain the sedum he must be very firm and insistent with his nurseryman to be supplied with the true sort, otherwise he will get a green-leaved object with a muddy pink inflorescence, not worth growing in anybody's garden. *Sedum telephium* 'Atropurpureum' is what he must insist on.

Veratrum nigrum is the other plant he may not know. It throws up a very sinister-looking spire, four to five feet high, tightly clustered with myriads of tiny, almost black, flowers, as though a swarm of bees or flying ants had settled all the way up the stem. Nobody could possibly describe it as pretty, but it has its interest and its

◆

Glowing *Eremurus bungei* with *Papaver commutatum* in the foreground.

somewhat perverse charm. It is very like a plate in some antique illustrated book, such as Thornton's *Temple of Flora*. It is to readers who appreciate Thornton's *Temple of Flora* that I recommend this queer, murky, murderous corner for their garden.

Acanthus spinosus

Murderous in two ways, because the root of *Veratrum nigrum* is poisonous; so be careful. A dark corner; a Mysteries of Udolpho corner; a corner that should be visited when the sky is lurid with an impending thunderstorm.

*U*SING ACANTHUS
The expression foliage plants carries something of a Victorian sound for us, like the echoing of a gong through a linoleumed, lincrustaed boarding-house, but in spite of this grim association some of the foliage plants hold a high decorative value in the garden. They fill up gaps in the border, and richly deserve to be called handsome.

I am thinking in particular of the acanthus. This is a plant with a classical tradition, for it provided Greek architects with the design for the Corinthian capital to their columns. The form of acanthus they used must have been *Acanthus spinosus*, or *spinosissimus*, which has dark green leaves and a most prickly spike of pale purple bracts, at least eighteen inches in length, very showy in July. For some odd reason it is popularly known as Bear's Breeches, though I should be sorry for any bear that had to wear them.

The form called *Acanthus*

mollis, or *mollis* 'Latifolius', has soft, rounded leaves of a paler green. It is less vicious than the spiny one, but on the whole I like the spiny one better.

Natives of the Mediterranean region, they naturally prefer a sunny place, but they will put up with a certain amount of shade. One is always grateful to plants that will consent to grow in that awkward corner where the sun penetrates only for a few hours during the day. Another obliging characteristic of the acanthus is that it will do very well as a plant in tubs or big pots, which you can stand about at your pleasure wherever you need them, on paths, or on steps, or on a terrace, or on any angle that the design of your garden suggests.

Finally, I must report the lasting property of its flowers in water. Recently, we sent some bits up to the local flower show – "three perennials in a vase". They came back to me, having duly won a prize, and not knowing what to do with them I stuck them into water in a black urn, and there they still are, after three weeks. That is a lot to claim, but it is honest-to-God true.

*M*ADONNA LILIES

I would like to write something more about lilies, especially the madonna lily, *Lilium candidum*, whose bulbs ought to be planted in this month of August. Never having grown it successfully, I am the last person to preach about it, and my remarks must be taken as theoretical.

> *Where did Gabriel get a lily*
> *In the month of March?*

I once read, and have never forgotten, those two lines in a poem by Grace James. Wherever that bright Archangel found his lily, it was certainly not in the more ambitious sort of garden. It prefers the humbler home. There is an old tradition that the madonna lily throve best in cottage gardens because the housewife was in the habit of chucking out her pail of soap-suds all over the flower-bed. Curiously enough, this tradition is now confirmed by the advice that the young growth of these lilies should be sprayed with a lather of soft-soap and water, to prevent the disease called botrytis. Thus do these old-wives' tales sometimes justify themselves.

The madonna lily should be planted now without delay. There is a variety called 'Salonica' which is said to be more resistant to botrytis, but, whichever variety you plant, put in the bulbs so shallow as to rest almost on top of the soil, showing their noses. If you bury them too deep, they will have to shove themselves up in that wise way that plants have, knowing what suits them even better than we know, but this is giving them a lot of trouble and struggle which you might have spared them. So plant them shallow, and plant them as soon as they arrive; don't leave the bulbs lying about, to get dry. And, once planted, leave them alone. Don't dig them up to move them to another place. Let them stay put. They are not modern-minded, wanting to roam about; they are statically minded; they are fond of their home, once you have induced them to take to it.

The madonna lily is an exception to the general rule that lilies demand plenty of humus. It likes lime, which may take the form of old mortar rubble, and it likes a scratchy soil. This, again, confirms the old theory that part of their success in cottage gardens was due to the fact that the grit from the surface of the lanes blew over the hedge and worked its way into the ground. Even today, when few country lanes are tarred, this may still hold good, and I have known cottagers send out their little boys with a shovel and a box mounted on old pram wheels to collect grit for the garden. It is never wise to disregard the sagacity of those who do not learn their lore from books.

THE GREAT WHITE MAGNOLIA

The flowers of *Magnolia grandiflora* look like great white pigeons settling among dark leaves. This is an excellent plant for covering an ugly wall-space, being evergreen and fairly rapid of growth. It is not always easy to know what to put against a new red brick wall; pinks and reds are apt to swear, and to intensify the already-too-hot colour; but the cool green of the magnolia's glossy leaves and the utter purity of its bloom make it a safe thing to put against any background, however trying. Besides, the flower in itself is of such splendid beauty. I have just been looking into the heart of one. The texture of the petals is of a dense cream; they should not be called white; they are ivory, if you can imagine ivory and cream stirred into a thick paste, with all the softness and smoothness of youthful human flesh; and the scent, reminiscent of lemon, was overpowering.

There is a theory that magnolias do best under the protection of a north or west wall, and this is true of the spring-flowering kinds, which are only too liable to damage from morning sunshine after a frosty night, when you may come out after breakfast to find nothing but a lamentable tatter of brown suède; but *grandiflora*, flowering in July and August, needs no such consideration. In fact, it seems to do better on a sunny exposure, judging by the two plants I have in my garden. I tried an experiment, as usual. One of them is against a shady west wall, and never carries more than half a dozen buds; the other, on a glaring south-east wall, normally carries twenty to thirty. The reason, clearly, is that the summer sun is necessary to ripen the wood on which the flowers will be borne. What they don't like is drought when they are young, i.e., before their roots have had time to go far in search of moisture; but as they will quickly indicate their disapproval by beginning to drop their yellowing leaves, you can be on your guard with a can of water, or several cans, from the rainwater butt.

Wires should be stretched along the wall on vine-eyes for convenience of future tying. This will save a lot of trouble in the long run, for the magnolia should eventually fill a space at least twenty feet wide by twenty feet high or more, reaching right up to the eaves of the house. The time may come when you reach out of your bedroom window to pick a great ghostly flower in the summer moonlight, and then you will be sorry if you find it has broken away from the wall and is fluttering on a loose branch, a half-captive pigeon trying desperately to escape.

SCENTED OLD ROSES

Whatever differences of opinion we may hold about roses, and whether our

taste inclines to the hybrid teas, or to the ramblers or to the old shrub roses, there is one thing on which we are all in agreement: it is an advantage for a rose to smell like a rose. The accusation is often brought against what people loosely call "modern roses" that they have lost their scent, an accusation sometimes but not always justified. 'Charles Mallerin', for instance, that magnificent black-red hybrid tea, dates back only ten years and is as rich in scent as it is in colour. I recall also, and still grow, a huge pink climber called 'Colcestria' which won the competition for the best-scented rose somewhere back in the 1920s; I cannot find it listed in any catalogue now, which seems a pity as it is not only powerfully scented but is what nurserymen describe as "vig".

There are roses which are "fast of their scent", requiring to be held to the nose, and others which generously spread themselves upon the summer air. Of these, I would signal three in particular: *Rosa rugosa* 'Alba' and the hybrid *rugosa* 'Blanc Double de Coubert', and the hybrid musk 'Penelope'. These all make big bushes, and should be placed near a corner where you frequently pass. They all have the merit of continuous flowering, and *rugosa* 'Alba' produces bright red hips in autumn, like little round apples amongst the yellowing leaves, adding to its attraction, interest and charm.

The *rugosa* hybrid, 'Parfum de l'Hay', has the reputation of being one of

Magnolia grandiflora

Rosa 'Souvenir du Docteur Jamain'

the most strongly scented of all roses. Unfortunately its constitution is not as strong as its scent. Perhaps light soils don't suit it. Its companion, 'Roseraie de l'Hay', might do better, and smells nearly as good. Neither of them makes a big bush, so would be suitable for a small garden.

'Souvenir du Docteur Jamain' is an old hybrid perpetual which I am rather proud of having rescued from extinction. I found him growing against the office wall of an old nursery. No one knew what he was; no one seemed to care; no one knew his name; no one had troubled to propagate him. Could I dig him up, I asked? Well, if you like to risk it, they said, shrugging their shoulders: it's a very old plant, with a woody stiff root. I risked it; 'Docteur Jamain' survived his removal; and now has a flourishing progeny in my garden and also on the market of certain rosarians to whom I gave him. 'Dr Jamain' is a deep red, not very large flowers, but so sweetly and sentimentally scented. Some writers would call it nostalgically scented, meaning everything that burying one's nose into the heart of a rose meant in one's childhood, or in one's adolescence when one first discovered poetry, or the first time one fell in love.

I think 'Dr Jamain' should not be planted in too sunny a place. He burns. A south-west aspect suits him better than full south.

PLANTS FOR SHADY PLACES

People often ask what plants are suitable for a shady situation, by which they mean either the north side of a wall or house, or in the shadow cast by trees. There are so many such plants that no one need despair. A number of shrubby things will do well, such as the azaleas, the kalmias, the rhododendrons, and a pretty, seldom seen, low-growing shrub with waxy white pendant flowers called *Zenobia pulverulenta,* always provided that the soil is lime-free for all these subjects. The many cotoneasters and berberis have no objection to shade, and are less pernickety as to soil. *Daphne laureola* will thrive, and so will *Viburnum burkwoodii,* very easy and sweet-scented, making a big bush.

The well-known snowberry, *Symphoricarpos racemosus,* will grow anywhere and is attractive in autumn with its ivory berries and tangle of black twigs. And if you want something more choice than the snowberry, there are many magnolias which enjoy the protection of a north wall: *M. soulangiana,* white; *M. soulangiana* 'Lennei', wine-pink; and *M. liliiflora* 'Nigra', a deep claret colour, which has the advantage of a very long flowering season, all through May and June, with a few odd flowers appearing even in July and August. The magnolias all appreciate some peat or leaf-mould to fill in the hole you dig out when you plant them, and it is important not to let them suffer from drought before they have had time to become established.

If, however, you have no space for these rather large shrubs, there are plenty of things other than shrubs to fill up an un-sunny border. There are the foxgloves, which can now be obtained in varieties far superior to the woodland foxglove, flowering all round the stem, and in colours preferable to the old magenta, lovely though that may look in the woods. The hellebores and the lily-of-the-valley, the primroses and the polyanthus, the candelabra primulas, and, as you grow more ambitious, the blue poppy *Meconopsis baileyi,* which is the dream of every gardener, will all take happily to a shaded home, especially if some moisture keeps them fresh.

September

Pack the dark fibre in the potter's bowl;
Set bulbs of hyacinth and daffodil,
Jonquil and crocus, (bulbs both sound and whole),
Narcissus and the blue Siberian squill.
Set close, but not so tight
That flow'ring heads collide as months fulfil
Their purpose, and in generous sheaf expand
Obedient to th'arrangement of your hand.
Yours is the forethought, yours the sage control.

The Garden

SEPTEMBER SHELTERS

September.... What a turnover, what a watershed of the year. I always think of the months in terms of our own human decades: April-May; June-July; August-September. From March to the end of April is youth; from May to June is middle youth, up to one's thirtieth birthday, that disagreeable milestone; from June to July is the stage between thirty and forty, or should we say fifty? It is perhaps kinder to say fifty; but after the end of July we enter upon the painful stage when we know we are going on for sixty; and then comes September, when we approach seventy; and then comes October and November and December, when it would be tactless to pursue the analogy any further.

By September we ought to start thinking about the rough windswept days to come. Cold winds can sear a plant as surely as fire, but I fancy that we could go a long way towards frustrating their attack by the use of what we in Kent call hop-lewing. Lew is a nice little, old little word meaning shelter. It is probably most familiar in its nautical connection, but I like the countryman's use of it: "The lambs 'ud 'ave bin froze if so be I 'adn't made a few lews".

Hop-lewing is a very loosely woven grey canvassy sort of material, which hop-growers set up on tall poles on the windy side of their hop-gardens. It is six feet wide, and is sold in long strips of fifty yards. I can see no reason why we should not employ it, cut into suitable lengths, in our gardens. No need to set it up on tall poles. We should stretch it at ground level, fastened to stakes at intervals. The loose openness of the weave would allow for the free passage of air, so necessary to all plants, and so often prevented with fatal results by the denser packing of hurdles

Venidio-arctotis growing outside the door of the South Cottage.

stuffed with straw and bracken, or by the thick covering in which some people swathe their treasures throughout the winter, as in a warm dressing-gown.

An elongated ghost of hop-lewing, a grey ghost put through a mangle. That is what my garden is going to be haunted by next winter.

A COTTAGE HYDRANGEA

I know I am continuously grousing about the dearth of plants, apart from annuals and herbaceous stuff, to enliven the garden in August and September, so it was with a startled pleasure that I observed three bushes growing in a cottage garden as I drove along a secret lane. They looked like pink lilac. Tall, pyramidal in shape, smothered in pointed panicles of flower, they suggested a bush of pink lilac in May. Yet this was September. . . . Puzzled, I stopped by the roadside to investigate.

It was *Hydrangea paniculata* 'Grandiflora', sometimes called the plumed hydrangea. In its native country, Japan, it is said to attain a height of 25 feet, but in this country it apparently limits itself to something between six and eight feet; and quite enough, too, for the average garden. Do not confuse it with the hortensia hydrangea, the one which sometimes comes sky-blue but more often a dirty pink, and which is the one usually seen banked up in Edwardian opulence against the grandstand of our more fashionable race-courses. *H. paniculata* 'Grandiflora', in spite of its resounding name, is less offensively sumptuous and has a far subtler personality.

It reveals, for instance, a sense of humour, and even of fantasy in the colouring it adopts throughout its various stages. It starts off by flowering white; then turns into the pink I have already described as looking like pink lilac, which I know I ought to call syringa, but somehow lilac, or even laylock, comes easier to my pen. Then it turns greenish, a sort of sea-green, so you never know where you are with it, as you never know where you are with some human personalities, but that makes them all the more interesting. Candidly white one moment; prettily pink the next; and virulently green in the last resort. . . . As I was leaning over the gate, looking at this last pink-green inflorescence, the tenant of the cottage observed me and came up. Yes, he said, it has been in flower for the last three months. It changes its colour as the months go by, he said. He knew it was a hydrangea, though he couldn't remember its second name. He was very proud of it. He was a dark man, a foreigner; and although he spoke fluent English he had a thick, peculiar accent which I could not identify. As I was talking to him across his gate, a circus passed with all its caravans and roundabouts; and I thought that the foreign man, and the circus, and the English country garden were all very much of the same thing; and that I would certainly order *H. paniculata* 'Grandiflora' to grow in a damp, shady spot next year in my garden.

SCARLET CAMPION

Some two years ago I observed a brilliant showy plant growing in the prettiest of Scottish nursery gardens. I long to go back there. The garden had been carved out of a clearing in a wood of silver birch and dark green juniper; many little burns ran down channels cut in the peaty soil; primulas and gentians grew like weeds, though true weeds there were none. It was not only the prettiest but also the tidiest of nursery gardens, crammed with covetable things which I feared I could not grow with any success down here in the south-east of England.

I did, however, bring away a pot-grown plant of *Lychnis haageana*, the showy brilliant plant I referred to; and it has served me well. I would recommend it to everybody who wants a flare of colour for the front of the border or for the rock garden in July. I saved its seed, but need scarcely have troubled to do so, as it came up of its own accord in unexpected places, a most agreeable device for a plant which, although nominally a perennial is apt to die out after a year or so. My original plant hasn't, yet, but has left so profuse a progeny that its departure into another world would not now matter, except that one is always sorry to say goodbye.

This would be the time to obtain ripe seed for sowing. I must warn prospective growers that this campion, the English name for lychnis, is variable when you grow it from seed. The seeds I saved and sowed threw flowers in different colours. Some of them came in the bright orange red of the flame of an oil-lamp, *lychnos* being the Greek word for a lamp. Some of them came much paler, straw-coloured; some came pale pink; and some a dull white. I scrapped the white; threw them out; kept the straw-coloured and the pink and left the rest to seed themselves and take a chance on their coming up in the show they will make, as I hope, next year.

They are rather untidy; their leaves are ugly; their flowers shaggy and tattered like a flag torn in a gale. But so gay, even as a flag flying twelve inches above the ground. Truly, they are worth this recommendation. They got an Award of Merit from the R.H.S. in 1953, which is something worth having, a more valuable sanction than I could give.

Campions all, they belong to the same family as the ragged robin of our banks and woodlands, and as the tall, scarlet, rather coarse *Lychnis chalcedonica* so familiar once in old herbaceous borders and still not to be despised.

CLIMBERS AND RAMBLERS

In September, many climbing roses begin their second season of flower. Not all of the best climbers are so generous, and I do not think we should choose our varieties solely because they will flower twice. Many of the most vigorous growers would then be excluded, yet they are the best for special assignments, whether we plant over a bank, or up a pillar, or over an archway, or in that most graceful fashion of sending the long strands up into an old tree, there to soar and dangle, loose and untrammelled.

The rambling wichuraianas are especially suited for

Lychnis haageana

such a purpose, since with one or two exceptions such as 'Albertine' and 'Albéric Barbier' they are apt to develop mildew on a wall, and prefer the air to blow freely through them. 'Félicité et Perpétué', commemorating two young women who suffered martyrdom at Carthage in A.D. 203, will grow at least twenty feet high into the branches, very appropriately, since St. Perpetua was vouchsafed the vision of a wonderful ladder reaching up to heaven. 'François Juranville' and 'Léontine Gervais', both pink-and-buff, hang prettily, if less vigorous of growth. Among other wichuraianas, of a stiffer character than the ramblers, 'New Dawn' and 'Dr. Van Fleet' are to my mind two of the best, very free-flowering throughout the summer, of a delicate but definite rose-pink. 'Emily Gray', reputed tender though I have never found her so, planted on a south-facing wall, large single pale yellow flowers, and dark green shiny leaves; 'Cupid', a hybrid tea, pink with a gold central boss; and 'Elegance', white and gold, are all very much to be recommended. 'Mermaid' is perhaps too well known to be mentioned, but should never be forgotten, partly for the sake of the pale-yellow flowers, opening flat and single, and partly because of the late flowering season, which begins after most other climbers are past their best. I should add that 'Mermaid' should be regarded with caution by dwellers in cold districts.

Where the choice is so wide it becomes difficult to include all that certainly deserve inclusion, but I must mention 'Allen Chandler', a magnificent red,

Rosa 'Paul Neyron'

only semi-double, which carries some bloom all through the summer. Not, I think, a rose for a house of new brick, but superb on grey stone, or on white-wash, or indeed any colour-wash. If you want a white rose, flushed pink, very vigorous and seldom without flowers, try 'Mme Alfred Carrière', best on a sunny wall but tolerant of a west or even a north aspect; and if a yellow rose, very deep yellow, plant 'Lawrence Johnston', of which it must, however, be said that the first explosion of bloom is not usually succeeded by many subsequent flowers.

Finally, remember that many of the hybrid teas may be obtained in climbing forms, including the in-my-opinion horridly coarse but ever-popular 'Peace'.

PEGGING PERPETUAL ROSES

The bourbon roses gave birth to the race of hybrid perpetuals, which in their turn were developed into the hybrid teas. The hybrid perpetuals have now become somewhat obsolete and superseded by the hybrid teas, a pity in my opinion since there are still some H.P.s available and some of them are very useful for prolonging the season besides having the quality of lasting well in water.

This is especially true of 'Ulrich Brunner', stiff-stemmed, almost thornless, cherry-red in colour, very prolific indeed, a real cut-and-come-again.

These strong growers lend themselves to various ways of treatment. They can be left to reach their free height of seven to eight feet, but then they wobble about over eye-level and you can't see them properly, with the sun in your eyes, also they get shaken by summer gales. A better but more laborious system is to tie them down to benders, by which I mean flexible wands of hazel with each end poked firmly into the ground and the rose-shoots tied down at intervals, making a sort of half-hoop.

This entails a lot of time and trouble, but it is satisfactory if you can do it; also it means that the rose breaks at each joint, so that you get a very generous floraison. If you decide to grow hybrid perpetuals on this system of pegging them down, you ought to feed them richly, with organic manure if you can get it, or with compost if you make it, but anyhow with something that will compensate for the tremendous effort they will put out from being encouraged to break all along their shoots. You can't ask everything of a plant, any more than you can exact everything of a human being, without giving some reward in return. Even the performing seal gets an extra herring. 'Ulrich Brunner', 'Frau Karl Druschki', and the 'Dicksons', 'Hugh' and 'George', are very suitable for this kind of training.

The hybrid perpetuals can also be used as wall plants; not nearly so tall as true climbers and ramblers, they are quite tall enough for, say, a space under a ground floor window; or they may be grown on post-and-wire as espaliers outlining a path. I once had a blood-red 'Dickson' trained in the shape of a peacock's tail.

I find 'Paul Neyron' described in one rosarian's catalogue as having "the largest flowers we know among roses . . . suffused with an exquisite shade of lilac, with silver reverse", and in another catalogue as having "enormous rich pink flowers, fully double". This sounds all right to me; I have long since learnt not to be misled by catalogue descriptions, but these are from two catalogues that I can trust. Moreover, 'Paul Neyron' appears to be identical with, or indistinguishable from, the famous

'Rose de la Reine', raised in 1840 by M. Laffay, of Auteuil, who grew 200,000 seedling roses a year and took his chance of finding something really good amongst them.

That gives one to think.

MOUNTAIN ORACH

Many people have told me, and many gardening articles have reported, that the seeds of annuals have shown very poor germination during 1958; in plain English they haven't come up. I don't know the explanation; perhaps they simply rotted in the ground or were washed away as seedlings or were splashed flat into mud by rain. Whatever the reason the result was distressingly negative. But one rather unusual annual did not let me down. This was the mountain orach (*Atriplex hortensis* 'Rubra').

Occasionally it is borne in upon me that my taste in flowers may be peculiar. Some people, invited to admire my mountain orach, said it reminded them of nothing so much as Irish widows keening round a grave; others said it reminded them of wet umbrellas standing unfurled to drip in the porch of a seaside boarding-house; and a visitor from the tropics went so far as to say it reminded him of those giant bats called flying foxes which hang upside down like derelict mackintoshes draping the tops of high trees in Indonesia.

I remain obstinately pleased with my mountain orach. I dare say it does look a bit disconsolate as it sags downwards sodden with rain. (A stake would have corrected this, but one can't spare the time to go round staking everything that needs it.) Still I protest that it has served me well. I protest also that it isn't nearly as black and dismal as an umbrella, but is of a deep rich purple in the leaf, darker than a Cardinal's robes, and that its seeding-heads now forming suggest the colour of porphyry. Or rubies.

Perhaps I have not made out a very good case for my mountain orach. I ought to add that it is very useful to pick for indoors; lasts well in water; and combines very well with the gladiolus called 'Uhu' – a smoky-mauve. Finally, if you don't take kindly to it as a decorative plant in the garden you can always chop it down and eat it. It is a sort of spinach.

HARDIER THAN YOU THINK

Some plants suffer from a reputation for tenderness long years before we realise that they are far hardier than was supposed. A classic example is the alstroemeria, which according to an old catalogue in my possession, dated 1838, was regarded as a subject for the hothouse. We know better now.

I have in mind the climber, *Eccremocarpus scaber*. I was brought up to consider it not only "difficult" but half-hardy, and then it got itself into my garden where it became an ineradicable weed, surviving even the terrible winter of 1946-47. I tore it out by the handful; it always reappeared, so in face of such devotion I had to give in, and it has now smothered poor 'Miss Jessop's Upright' rosemary to such good purpose that 'Miss Jessop' is no longer green and upright, but orange-red and couchant to the ground.

The eccremocarpus is not one of my favourite climbers; visitors to my garden, however, appear to like it and often ask what it is. That is why I mention it here. It has its merits. It produces a quantity of its waxy, orange, tubular flowers in late July and August and September, always a rather colourless time in the garden. It produces also an enormous quantity of seed-pods, which may be harvested and sown next spring under glass in the same way as you would sow morning glory (*Ipomoea*) or *Cobaea scandens*, to cover a trellis or a porch. These rapid growers are so useful. The eccremocarpus, like the cobaea, will grow ten feet and more in one summer season.

I can imagine also that eccremocarpus would make a pleasing pot-plant, treated as an annual, and wiggled up and around some bamboo sticks. I offer this suggestion to town-gardeners or to all gardeners who have not much space room on the ground level. Pots can be stood about anywhere in odd corners. I know they need watering, but that is just the penalty one has to pay for growing plants in pots or tubs. One can't have everything for nothing.

LIGHT-COLOURED LEAVES

I have never yet made up my mind about plants of variegated foliage. There was a time when I was arrogantly certain that I did not like them: could not abide them; was reminded of Victorian shrubberies; even of aspidistras in sea-side lodging-houses. Such are the powers of association.

Now, I am not so sure. One's taste alters; but whether it ameliorates or deteriorates is difficult to determine. There can be no Absolute in canons of taste; there are only standards, and although these should always be high they should never remain rigid. Mine, so far as concerns variegated foliage, are still in a state of flux. They waver, as reeds in a stream, but at least the stream is frisky and not stagnant.

These reflections have been unwittingly suggested to me by a correspondent who asks what things with "light-coloured leaves" he could plant in his garden. I see what he means. He wants a silvery-looking small tree; let him plant the silver maple, *Acer saccharinum*.

There are many other maples, scarlet of leaf, only too familiar in small rock gardens; I can see

Eccremocarpus scaber

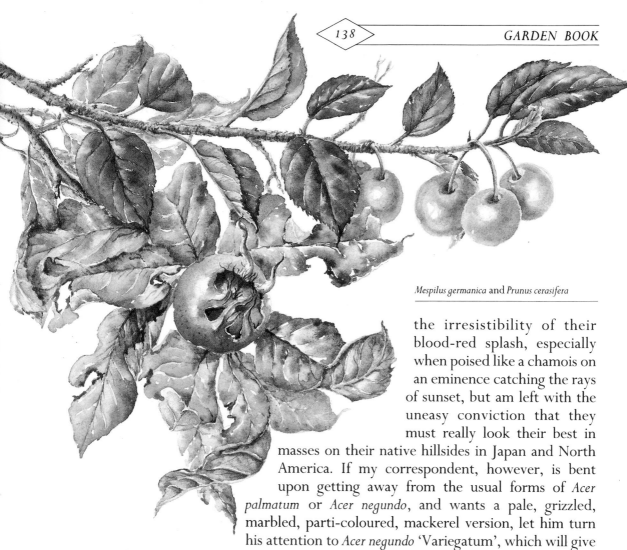

Mespilus germanica and *Prunus cerasifera*

the irresistibility of their blood-red splash, especially when poised like a chamois on an eminence catching the rays of sunset, but am left with the uneasy conviction that they must really look their best in masses on their native hillsides in Japan and North America. If my correspondent, however, is bent upon getting away from the usual forms of *Acer palmatum* or *Acer negundo*, and wants a pale, grizzled, marbled, parti-coloured, mackerel version, let him turn his attention to *Acer negundo* 'Variegatum', which will give green leaves with a white edging, or *A. negundo* 'Auratum' which as its name implies gives leaves splotched with yellow. Any of these can be planted in little groups or as single specimens; some peat in the soil pleases them, and it is well to keep them away from frost if possible, not because of any tenderness in their constitution but because the young leaves are liable to damage from frost or cold winds, making them look seared and shabby.

If it is not necessarily variegation that my correspondent requires, but merely a pale tree, he might try *Pyrus salicifolia* 'Pendula'. This is otherwise known as the willow-leafed pear, very grey, with white flowers in April, and a drooping habit not unlike a weeping willow. It should definitely be grown as a single specimen, preferably in a place where you can walk all round it and admire its circularity. Extremely graceful, the tips of its long shoots can be clipped to prevent them from trailing on the ground.

CHERRY PLUMS

The medlar is not a fruit I care much about; by the time it is ready to eat, it bears far too close a resemblance to a rotting or "bletted" pear. It can, however, be made into a preserve, and the little tree certainly has a definite garden value, for in a favourable autumn the leaves turn into a motley of very beautiful variegated colours – pink, yellow, green, and brown, freckled with the russet fruits which always remind me of those knobbly objects you see attached to leather thongs on the flail-like hand-weapons of medieval warfare.

But although I may have no great affection for the medlar as a fruit, my affection for the cherry plum or myrobalan knows no bounds. I wish it could be planted more lavishly. It has every virtue. It grows quickly; it is pretty in the spring, with its white blossom; it reaches its supreme beauty when its fruit ripens in mid-summer and its branches droop with the weight of fruit almost to the ground. The branches then seem loaded with fat jewels of amber and topaz, like a tree in an oriental fairy-tale.

It crops generously, most years. Its fruit makes delicious jam, especially if you put in the kernels of the stones, when you get a sharp almond flavour reminding you of kernels left in apricot jam. It is, I feel sure, a tree to plant both for your immediate pleasure and for the pleasure of your children after you.

Plant the gages, too. The old greengage and all the other gages. This is the time to order and plant them.

UPRIGHT YEWS

A full-stop or exclamation mark is often of extreme importance in a garden, something which will arrest the eye and give emphasis to some focal point. For this purpose nothing could be more effective than the Irish yew, which with its erect fastigiate habit may well be considered as taking the place of the cypress in this country. It can be kept as neat and slender as any cypress, for many years, by a judicious tying-in of its branches from early youth until it reaches its eventual height of some twenty feet or more. Even when quite young, only five or six feet high, the little pointed tree looks agreeably mature, an impression doubtless due to the sobriety of its dark attire and the serious uprightness of its demeanour.

Is the story of its origin too well-known to bear repetition? It seems to have appeared as a chance seedling of our common native yew, *Taxus baccata*, and was found nearly 200 years ago by a Mr Willis on his farm in the hills of Co. Fermanagh. Mr Willis was shrewd enough to notice the difference. He retained one of his two seedlings and gave the other to his landlord at Florence Court where it still survives, the matriarchal ancestress of any Irish yew now awaiting your order in a nursery garden. The well-informed reader may here object that some young trees were found growing wild in Sussex in the first decade of this century, when nobody knew how they had come there, but these were male trees and who can say they were not a garden escape?

It may be useful to remark, for the benefit of those who grow yews or a yew hedge in their garden and who have observed a distressing sooty blackness spreading over their trees, that this dirty infection is readily curable by spraying in September and March with an emulsion of white oil and nicotine. It is due to a scale insect, which may be discovered as a tiny brown patch on the underside of the leaves and whose excrement produces the mould rightly named sooty mould, for you might as well handle the gear of a chimney-sweep. The excrement itself is known as honeydew; sad that so lovely a word should be afflicted with so unsavoury a meaning.

The scale should be got rid of as quickly as possible, and if the yews have already suffered to any serious extent they should be fed back into health. Dried blood is excellent, or you can dust round each plant with a handful of nitrate of soda, mixed with sand, in April, May, or June. This should perhaps be regarded as a stimulant rather than a food. Do not allow the mixture to touch either the stem or the leaves.

GOOD GROUPING

The more I see of other people's gardens the more convinced do I become of the value of good grouping and shapely training. These remarks must necessarily apply most forcibly to gardens of a certain size, where sufficient space is available for large clumps or for large specimens of individual plants, but even in a small garden the spotty effect can be avoided by massing instead of dotting plants here and there.

It is a truly satisfactory thing to see a garden well schemed and wisely planted. Well-schemed is the operative word. Every garden, large or small, ought to be planned from the outset, getting its bones, its skeleton, into the shape that it will preserve all through the year even after the flowers have faded and died away. Then, when all colour has gone, is the moment to revise, to make notes for additions and even to take the mattock for removals. This is gardening on the large scale, not in details. There can be no rules in so fluid and personal a pursuit, but it is safe to say that a sense of substance and solidity can be achieved only by the presence of an occasional mass breaking the more airy companies of the little flowers.

What this mass shall consist of must depend upon many things: upon the soil, the aspect, the colour of neighbouring plants, and above all upon the taste of the owner. I can imagine, for example, a border arranged entirely in purple and mauve – phlox, stocks, pansies, *Clematis jackmanii* trained over low hoops – all planted in bays between great promontories of the plum-coloured sumach, *Cotinus coggygria* 'Foliis Purpureis', but many people, thinking this too mournful, might prefer a scheme in red and gold. It would be equally easy of accomplishment, with a planting of the feathery *Thalictrum flavum glaucum,* gaillardias, *Achillea filipendulina* (the flat-headed yellow yarrow), helenium, *Lychnis chalcedonica*, and a host of other ordinary, willing herbaceous things. In this case, I suppose, the mass would have to be provided by bushes of something like the golden privet or the golden yew, both of which I detest when planted as "specimens" on a lawn, but which in so aureate a border would come into their own.

The possibilities of variation are manifold, but on the main point one must remain adamant: the alternation between colour and solidity, decoration and architecture, frivolity and seriousness. Every good garden, large or small, must have some architectural quality about it; and, apart from the all-important question of the general lay-out, including hedges, the best way to achieve this imperative effect is by heavy lumps of planting such as I have suggested.

I wish only that I could practise in my own garden the principles which I so complacently preach, week after week.

NATIVE JUNIPERS

It occurred to me, after writing about the Irish yew, that some people nourish a prejudice against yews. They think them funereal. This is purely a question of association, because yews are often found in churchyards, but people have their prejudices, and it is no good arguing against them.

A man convinced against his will, is of the same opinion still, so if people don't like the dark yew in their garden let me suggest a substitute, the Irish juniper, *Juniperus communis* 'Hibernica' or 'Stricta' which possesses the same rigid columnar shape, equally valuable as the full-stop or exclamation mark I recommended for a focal point, but less severe and grim, being blue-green, almost glaucous, in colour, not that dark- almost black-green that some people find so gloomy. Personally, I like all gloomy trees; perhaps I have a melancholy streak in my character; anyhow, I like the dark background they make, reminding me of cypresses in Italy and of stone pines in Spain.

The junipers have many advantages. For one thing, they are lime-lovers, meaning that owners of gardens on an alkaline chalky soil can plant them with every hope of success. This does not imply that they will not grow elsewhere: I have seen a creeping juniper, a spreading type, growing in peaty soil in Scotland, ramping wild all over a woodland stretch under silver birches. I brought home an armful of its dead branches, and used them as smouldering pokers to push into a wood-fire on my hearth, waving them about the room as one would wave old stalks of lavender or rosemary, redolent as incense but far fresher and less heavy on the air. I took this to be *J. horizontalis*, apparently the only variety which does not favour a limestone soil, but on inquiry discovered that it was the common juniper, dwarfed by deer and rabbits eating it in the winter.

It made a beautiful, stiff, dark carpet under the pallor of the silver birches. Little burns dribbled, in a natural irrigation. Their bubbles rose like bursting pearls over the

Cotinus coggygria 'Foliis Purpureis'

Solanum crispum

shallow pebbles. It made me wish to possess not a more-or-less formal but a completely informal garden, with wild woodland on the margin. I don't mean to complain about my own garden. It serves me and satisfies me quite well, except at the moments when I get into despair over it: very frequent moments, when I long to have some other sort of garden, quite different; a garden in Spain, a garden in Italy, a garden in Provence, a garden in Scotland.

WE ALL HAVE WALLS

The two great planting months, October and November, are close upon us, and those gardeners who desire the maximum of reward with the minimum of labour would be well advised to concentrate upon the flowering shrubs and flowering trees. How deeply I regret that fifteen years ago, when I was forming my own garden, I did not plant these desirable objects in sufficient quantity. They would by now be large and lavish instead of the shrubby, spindly infants I contemplate with impatience as the seasons come round.

That omission is one from which I would wish to save my fellow-gardeners, so, taking this opportunity, I implore them to secure trees and bushes from whatever nurseryman can still supply them: they will give far less trouble than the orthodox herbaceous flower, they will demand no annual division, many of them will require no pruning; in fact, all that many of them will ask of you is to watch them grow yearly into a greater splendour, and what more could be exacted of any plant?

Your choice will naturally depend upon the extent of your garden, but it should be observed that any garden, however small, has a house in it, and that that house has walls. This is a very important fact to be remembered. Often I hear people say, "How lucky you are to have these old walls; you can grow anything against them", and then when I point out that every house means at least four walls – north, south, east, and west – they say, "I never thought of that". Against the north and west sides you can grow magnolias or camellias; on the east side, which catches the morning sun, you can grow practically any of the hardy shrubs or climbers, from the beautiful ornamental quinces, commonly, though incorrectly called japonicas (the right name is chaenomeles), to the more robust varieties of ceanothus, powdery-blue, or a blue fringing on purple; on the south side the choice is even larger – a vine, for instance, will soon cover a wide, high space, and in a reasonable summer will ripen its bunches of small, sweet grapes (I recommend 'Royal Muscadine', if you can get it); or, if you want a purely decorative effect, the fast-growing *Solanum crispum* will reach to the eaves of the house and will flower in deep mauve for at least two months in early summer.

*O*CTOBER

There reigns a rusty richness everywhere;
See the last orange roses, how they blow
Deeper and heavier than in their prime,
In one defiant flame before they go;
See the red-yellow vine leaves, how they climb
In desperate tangle to the upper air;
So might a hoyden gipsy toss and throw
A scarf across her disobedient hair.
See the last zinnias, waiting for the frost,
The deadly touch, the crystals and the rime,
Intense of colour, violent, extreme,
Loud as a trumpet lest a note be lost
In blackened death that nothing can redeem.

The Garden

*T*HE PINKS OF AUTUMN

The autumn garden . . . It has its beauty; especially, perhaps, a garden with an old orchard attached to it. When I was very small, about four years old, I suppose, a line of poetry entered into my consciousness, never to leave it again:

Rye pappels drop about my head.

I had no idea what rye pappels might be, but they held a magic, an enchantment for me, and when in later life I identified them as the ripe apples of Andrew Marvell's poem they had lost nothing of their enchantment in the process of growing up.

Coming home from abroad, after an interval when the season had time to change from late summer into autumn, it struck me how pink and green the autumn garden was. Not bronze and blue, the colours we associate with the turning woods and the hazy distance and the blue smoke of bonfires along the hedgerows. The woods had not turned yet, but in the orchard the apples were rosy and in the garden the leaves of the paeonies were pink, and so were the leaves of the common azaleas, and so were the leaves of *Parrotia persica* and the leaves of that other little tree with the lovely name liquidambar, and the leaves of *Prunus sargentii*, so soon to drop, alas, from the row in which I had planted them along the top of a rosy-red brick retaining wall.

The naked, reddish stems of the belladonna lily (amaryllis) had shot up in that surprising way they have, and were opening their cluster of pink flowers. This is a bulbous plant well worth growing, for it is reasonably hardy in the open ground in a sunny, well-drained position, preferably at the foot of a wall, and it supplies flowers for picking at a time when choice-looking flowers are rare. What it likes is lots of

Aster × frikartii growing along a wall opposite the azaleas.

water in the early summer, while it is making its leaves, and then it likes to be left alone while the leaves disappear and nothing is seen until the flowering stems shoot up all of a sudden on an October morning.

The Michaelmas daisies were also rioting pink in my garden. All the sorts called Beechwood, 'Beechwood Charm', 'Beechwood Challenger', and that specially good one called 'Harrington's Pink'. Some people tell me that 'Harrington's Pink' is not a good doer. I can say only that it does very well here in ordinary conditions, and that I have no complaint to make against it. It thrives, adding its bit of brighter pink to the rich scale of colouring leaves in the incarnadine symphony of October.

*M*ISS PRESTON'S LILACS

In the last-minute scramble to order the shrubs we had made a note of in those far-away happy months of May and June, and have since forgotten, let us now remember the Preston lilacs, *Syringa prestoniae*, before it is too late.

I must confess I don't know anything about Miss Isabella Preston of Ottawa, beyond her name and her reputation as a hybridiser of lilacs and the exciting crosses she has made between *Syringa villosa* and *Syringa reflexa*. I wish I did know more. She must be one of those great gardeners, a true specialist devoting a whole life to the job – how enviable a decision to take, how wise to concentrate on one subject and to know everything about it instead of scattering little confetti bits of information over a hundred things. Such thoroughness and such privity of knowledge carry one back to medieval dates when leisure was the norm. I picture Miss Preston to myself as a lady in a big straw hat, going round with a packet of labels, a notebook, and a rabbit's tail tied to a bamboo stick.

Perhaps this is all wrong, but there can be nothing wrong about my impression of Miss Preston's lilacs. 'Elinor', which got an Award of Merit in 1951, is a most beautiful shrub with tall erect panicles of a deep rose colour, opening to a paler shade as is the habit of the whole *Syringa* family. 'Elinor' is the only one I have hitherto grown, and can give a personal testimonial to; but 'Isabella', another Award of Merit, is well spoken of, and so is 'Hiawatha', reddish-purple to start with, and pale rose to end up. All the Preston hybrids are said to be strong growers, and are also entirely hardy as one would expect from the harsh climate in which they have been raised. Whether you prefer them to the old garden lilac, in heavy plumes hanging wet with rain, or whether you will reject their looser delicacy in favour of those fat tassels with their faint scent associated with one's childhood, is for you to say.

*S*COTS ROSES

A word on the Burnet or Scots roses, so incredibly pretty, mottled and marbled, self-coloured and two-coloured, and moreover so easy to grow. As Mr Edward Bunyard did not fail to point out, there is no better covering for a dry bank, since they will not only bind it together with their dense root system, but will also run about underground and come up everywhere in a little thorny jungle or thicket, keeping the weeds away. They are also ideal plants for a poor starved soil or for a windy place where taller, less tough things might refuse to survive. Another of their

Syringa prestoniae 'Elinor'

virtues is that they will make a charming low hedge. Their one drawback, which one must admit to be serious, is that they flower only once a year; but their foliage is quite pleasant to the eye, and if they can be given a rough corner such as the dry bank suggested by Mr Bunyard, the brevity of their explosion in June may be forgiven them.

There is, however, an exception to this rule of short-lived flowering. 'Stanwell Perpetual' is its name. It is only half a Scot, being a hybrid between a Scot and a damask, or possibly a gallica; I like to think it has gallica blood in it, since France and Scotland have always enjoyed a curious affinity as exemplified by their pepper-pot architecture and by certain phrases which have passed from one language into the other: *Ne vous fachez pas, dinna fash yoursel*; and as for barley-sugar, or *sucre d'orge*, I could expand into a whole article over that.

This is by the way. The rose 'Stanwell Perpetual' is what I was writing about. I have become very fond of this modest rose, who truly merits the description perpetual. One is apt to overlook her during the great foison of early summer; but now in October, when every chosen flower is precious, I feel grateful to 'Stanwell Perpetual' for offering me her shell-pink, highly-scented, patiently-produced flowers, delicately doing her job again·for my delectation in a glass on my table, and filling my room with such a good smell that it puffs at me as I open the door.

'Stanwell Perpetual' grows taller than the average Scots rose. It grows four to five feet high. It is, as I have said, a hybrid. It has another name, according to Miss Nancy Lindsay, who is an expert on these old roses: the 'Victorian Valentine' rose. This evokes pictures of old Valentines – but, however that may be, I do urge you to plant 'Stanwell Perpetual' in your garden to give you a reward of picking in October.

SITTING AND THINKING

"Sometimes I sits and thinks, and sometimes I just sits". The practising gardener seldom finds time to do either. He, or she, is too busy weeding or staking or tying up things that have fallen over or have blown down, or cutting hedges, or planting bulbs for next spring. The major disadvantage of having a garden, and working in it, is that one leaves oneself with no leisure to study the result one has laboriously achieved, or more likely failed to achieve. The practising gardener is always a Martha; it is Mary who sits back in admiration, saying how pretty that looks! Mary thinks it has just happened, as a gift from heaven; Mary is a dreamer; practical pains and trouble that have gone to the making of the effect Mary admires. Mary can just sit. Martha, if she can spare the time for it, can and must sit and think.

This sitting-and-thinking is very valuable at this time of year. It is valuable at any time of year, in a garden, when you want to make notes on the mistakes and omissions you observe, but it is especially valuable in autumn, which is the time for shifting plants to other positions or ordering new plants from a nursery to fill up some gap you may now record. I spend quite a lot of time gazing round my garden and making notes of my mistakes and of my good intentions for the future. I sits and thinks, and I puts down the results of my thinks in a large notebook, under different headings which with any luck I shall remember to consult later on, a practice I would recommend to any fellow-gardener.

There are plants to be scrapped. I feel sure that one of the secrets of good gardening is always to remove, ruthlessly, any plant one doesn't like. Heartbreaking though it may be to chop down a tree one planted years ago, it is the right thing to do if that tree is now getting in the way and keeping the sun off something else that needs it. And so with everything: scrap what does not satisfy and replace it by something that will.

Aster × frikartii

I feel sure also that the autumn is the time to look closely at the shapes and forms of shrubs and trees in their setting. Even in the smallest garden there is probably some branch that would be better lopped off, some shrub that would look better with some discipline and control. Shape, in a garden, is so important, if you regard, as I think you should, gardening as an extension of architecture; in other words, your garden as an outdoor extension of your house.

SHEARING THE MICHAELMAS DAISY

I doubt whether anybody could emotionally love a Michaelmas daisy. The best that can be said for them is that they are indispensable, and that is saying a lot for anything or anybody. They are certainly indispensable if you want to have any show of colour in a border around the feast of St Michael the Archangel, which falls on September 29. They come out into their pretty colours of mauve, purple, red, and pink.

My object in writing this note on the aster we all grow in our gardens is to pass on a hint I was given last year. I took it, and am glad I did. I was worried by the straggly height my asters were growing to; I knew they ought to be staked or propped up in some way, but where was the time for staking or propping to be found, with so many more urgent jobs to do? A kindly scornful visitor came along. "Oh, surely you know that you ought to take the shears over them at the beginning of July and trim them back to within a couple of feet of ground level, as you might trim a hedge? Then, they will grow stout and sturdy, instead of lanky and leggy".

I took the advice, rather apprehensive as to the result. It worked. This autumn my Michaelmas daisies have been reasonably short of stature. They have not required staking; and on the whole I think this severe treatment has made them flower more densely than usual. Also they have been free from mildew, even after this unnaturally wet summer. There may be no connection between this and the shearing, but such is the fact.

SCHEMES FOR MIXED BORDERS

Plaintive letters reach me from time to time saying that if I do not like herbaceous borders what would I put in their place? It is quite true that I have no great love for herbaceous borders or for the plants that usually fill them – coarse things with no delicacy or quality about them. I think the only justification for such borders is that they shall be perfectly planned, both in regard to colour and to grouping; perfectly staked; and perfectly weeded. How many people have the time or the labour? The alternative is a border largely composed of flowering shrubs, including the big bush roses; but for those who still desire a mixed border it is possible to design one which will (more or less) look after itself once it has become established.

It could be carried out in various colour schemes. Here is an idea for one in red and purple and pink: floribunda roses 'Dusky Maiden' and 'Frensham'; musk roses 'Wilhelm', 'Pink Prosperity', 'Cornelia', 'Felicia'; the common old red herbaceous paeonies, with Darwin tulips planted amongst them if you like; and a front edging of

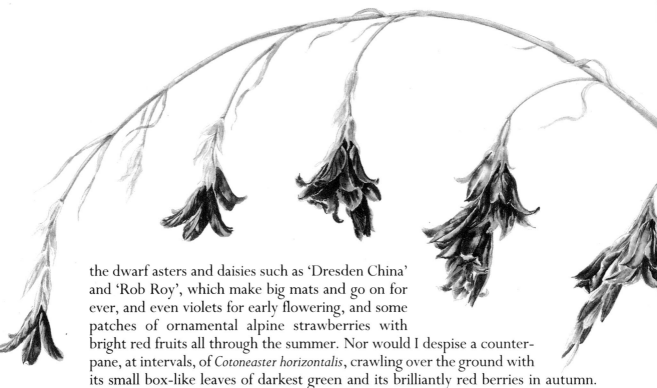

the dwarf asters and daisies such as 'Dresden China' and 'Rob Roy', which make big mats and go on for ever, and even violets for early flowering, and some patches of ornamental alpine strawberries with bright red fruits all through the summer. Nor would I despise a counterpane, at intervals, of *Cotoneaster horizontalis*, crawling over the ground with its small box-like leaves of darkest green and its brilliantly red berries in autumn.

Another idea, pale and rather ghostly, a twilight-moonlight border, Forsythia along the back; musk roses 'Danae', 'Moonlight' and 'Thisbe' in the middle; evening primroses, *Oenothera biennis*, self-sowing; *Iris ochroleuca*, tall and white and yellow; creamy paeonies; and a front carpet of silver-foliaged artemisias and stachys.

Of course, these are only the roughest indications, outlines to be filled in. The main thing, it seems to me, is to have a foundation of large, tough, untroublesome plants with intervening spaces for the occupation of annuals, bulbs, or anything that takes your fancy. The initial outlay would seem extravagant, but at least it would not have to be repeated, and the effect would improve with every year.

May I thank all the kind people who have sent me helpful letters, pencils, and samples of labels? I now have a wonderful collection of every shape, size, colour, and substance. I am most grateful, and regret only that I have not been able to acknowledge each letter separately.

*T*HE WAND FLOWER

When a thing is well known to oneself, one is apt to take for granted that it is equally familiar to other people, a grave error and a form of egotism which should be carefully suppressed. Thus, I have several times been surprised by inquiries about a plant which I supposed to be as ordinary as a primrose. Apparently it isn't. It attracts attention; it arouses curiosity; and it meets with approval.

The plant I have in mind is the wand flower, *Dierama pulcherrimum*. I would not, myself, describe the wand flower as most beautiful, because the flowers I like best are the flowers requiring a close inspection before they consent to reveal their innermost secret beauty, and the wand flower does not come up to so exacting a standard. One should not, however, demand from any plant or, indeed, from any person, qualities which by their nature they are precluded from giving.

The wand flower is an untidy grower. It comes up amongst a clump of reedy-looking leaves, wiry; and throws its wands of wine-coloured flowers in lovely curves, bending this way and that, never upright, and never still. This, to me, is the chief charm of the wand flower: it is always moving. Even on a breathless summer evening, when there is no stir in the leaves of the poplars, the wand flower is always faintly on the move. Its pendulous bells shake slightly. It is alive to an imperceptible breath.

Ideally, the wand flower should be grown near water. You would then get a duplication: the flower blown gently by the breeze and the flower reflected in the water, moving about within the ripples and going right down into apparently bottomless black depths. In such a position, moreover, the reed-like leaves would not look out of place as they do in a bed or a border, but do not make the mistake of thinking that dierama is a marsh-loving subject. On the contrary, it prefers a well-drained place, so in order to grow it near water you would have to plant it on an overhanging bank. A South African, it also loves the sun.

You will find that it demands a little patience before it becomes happily established, a year or two perhaps, but it does increase itself by seedlings and a very few corms will in time produce a satisfying clump. The colours are variable. A wine-red is the most usual, but it also comes in pink and white. It should be planted in October.

DEAR OLD DILL

May I put in a good word for dill? It is, I think, extremely pretty, both in the garden and picked for indoors, perhaps especially picked for indoors, where it looks like a very fine golden lace, feathery amongst the heavy flat heads of yarrow, *Achillea filipendulina*, one of the most usual herbaceous plants to be found in any garden.

Dill, of course, is not an herbaceous plant; it is an annual, but it sows itself so prolifically that one need never bother about its renewal. It sees to that for itself, and comes up year after year where you want it and in many places where you don't. It has many virtues, even if you do not rely upon it "to stay the hiccough, being boiled in wine", or to "hinder witches of their will". Amongst its virtues, apart from its light yellow grace in a mixed bunch of flowers, is the fact that you can

Dierama pulcherrimum

use its seeds to flavour vinegar, and for pickling cucumbers. You can also, if you wish, use the young leaves to flavour soups, sauces, and fish. All mothers know about dill-water, but few will want to go to the trouble of preparing that concoction for themselves, so on the whole the most practical use the cook or the housewife will find for this pretty herb lies in the harvest of its seeds, which are indistinguishable from caraway seeds in seed-cake or rolled into scones or into the crust of bread. Once she has got it going in her garden, she need never fear to be short of supply for seed cake, since one ounce is said to contain over twenty-five thousand seeds; and even if she has got a few seeds left over out of her thousands she can keep them waiting, for they will still be viable after three years.

The correct place for dill is the herb garden, but if you have not got a herb garden it will take a very decorative place in any border. I like muddling things up; and if a herb looks nice in a border, then why not grow it there? Why not grow anything anywhere so long as it looks right where it is? That is, surely, the art of gardening.

By the way, the official botanical name of dill is *Anethum graveolens*, for the information of anyone who does not prefer the short monosyllable, as I do.

BLADDER SENNAS

Two shrubs with an amazingly long flowering period are *Colutea arborescens* and *Colutea media*, the Bladder Sennas. They have been flowering profusely for most of the summer, and are still very decorative in the middle of October. Of the two, I prefer the latter which has coppery pea-shaped flowers; *C. arborescens* has yellow flowers; but although *media* is perhaps the more showy, they go very prettily together, seeming to complement one another in their different colouring. Graceful of growth with their long sprays of acacia-like foliage, amusingly hung with the bladders of seed-pods which give them their English name, the

Anethum graveolens

bright small flowers suggest swarms of winged insects. They are of the easiest possible cultivation, doing best in a sunny place, and having a particular value in that they may be used to clothe a dry bank where few other things would thrive, nor do they object to an impoverished stony soil, in fact they like it. They are easy to propagate, either by cuttings or by seed, and they may be kept shapely by pruning in February, within a couple of inches of the old wood.

There is also *Colutea orientalis*, which I confess I have never seen. This has the same coppery flowers as *C. media*, itself a hybrid of *arborescens* and *orientalis*, but is said to be less generous of its flowers and to depend for its charm chiefly on the grey or glaucous quality of its leaf. One might try them all three, especially in a rough place. I know that highbrow gardeners do not consider them as very choice. Does that matter? To my mind they are delicately elegant, and anything which will keep on blooming right into mid-October has my gratitude.

By the way, they are not the kind of which you can make senna-tea. Children may thus regard them without suspicion and will need little encouragement to pop the seed-pods. It is as satisfactory as popping fuchsias.

A RAMPANT CLIMBER

Very often one is asked to suggest a climber which will rapidly cover an unsightly shed or fence. All too often one falls back on the Russian vine with the unwieldy name *Polygonum baldschuanicum*. This is undoubtedly a useful thing, and if one remembers its romantic place of origin, Bokhara, one may possibly contemplate its fluffy heads with increased affection, but even this suggestion of central Asian mystery cannot greatly endear it to the lover of garden beauty.

I would propose as a substitute *Akebia quinata* or *Akebia trifoliata*, sometimes called *Akebia lobata*. They both come from China and Japan, and are as vigorous as the most impatient coverer of sheds or fences could wish. I happen to live in a somewhat unusual house which includes a tall tower, with a fire-escape ladder up it. I would defy anybody to ascend that ladder now that an akebia has taken possession of it. Of course if you want a showy climber, such as a clematis, you will not get it in the akebias. Their flowers are rather subtle in colouring, chocolate-

Colutea media

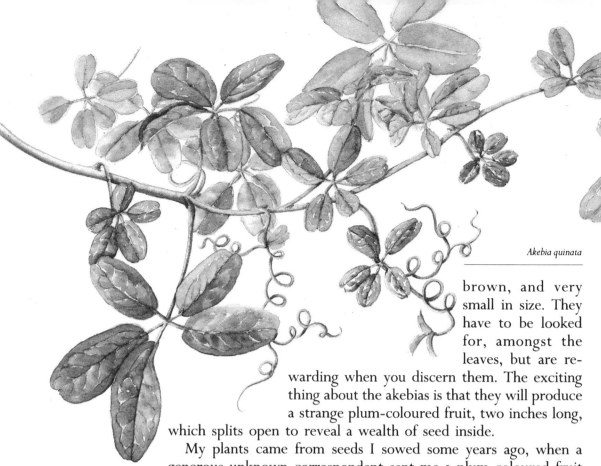

Akebia quinata

brown, and very small in size. They have to be looked for, amongst the leaves, but are rewarding when you discern them. The exciting thing about the akebias is that they will produce a strange plum-coloured fruit, two inches long, which splits open to reveal a wealth of seed inside.

My plants came from seeds I sowed some years ago, when a generous unknown correspondent sent me a plum-coloured fruit from her garden in Cheshire. It was a beautiful fruit, splitting open to expose masses of seed apparently wrapped in damp grey cotton-wool. I dried it off, and to my surprise every seed germinated, giving me more plants than I knew what to do with. This was *Akebia trifoliata*, whose purple fruits dangle now in clusters like huge grapes from the trellised roof the plant has smothered.

A year or so ago, an article appeared in the Journal of the Royal Horticultural Society advising hand-pollination if fruits were to be obtained. It may be of interest if I here record the result of following this advice. There are three plants of akebia growing in my garden; the one smothering the fire-escape is *Akebia quinata*; the other two are *Akebia trifoliata*. *Akebia quinata* was left to its own devices. It flowered, but did not fruit. Of the other two, *trifoliata*, one was hand-pollinated, the other not. The hand-pollinated one carried about a dozen fruits, the other one a slightly larger quantity. Explain it as you will.

The moral seems to be that this climber is well worth growing, for its rapid growth, its density of leaf, its attractive little chocolate-coloured flowers, and its plummy waxy fruits when it consents to produce them. As I like to be honest, however, I must add that when I rather proudly exhibited these fruits to a friend, she said they reminded her of a very expensive cake of soap.

OUR NATIVE IRIS

A spike of the brightest orange caught my eye, half hidden by a clump of *Berberis thunbergii* which had turned very much the same colour. They were both of an extraordinary brilliance in the low afternoon sunshine. I could not remember if I had planted them deliberately in juxtaposition, or if they had come together by a fortunate chance. Investigation revealed further spikes: three-sided seed-pods cracked wide open to expose the violent clusters of the berries within.

This was our native *Iris foetidissima* in its autumn dress, our only other native iris being the yellow waterside flag, *I. pseudacorus*. No one would plant *I. foetidissima* for the sake of its name, which in English is rendered the stinking iris and derives from the unpleasant smell of the leaves if you bruise them. There is, however, no need to bruise leaves, a wanton pastime, and you can call it the gladdon or gladwyn iris if you prefer, or even the roast-beef plant. Some etymologists think that gladdon or gladwyn are corruptions of gladiolus, owing to a similarity between the sword-like leaves; but I wish someone would tell me how it got its roast-beef name.

The flowers, small, and of a dingy mauve, are of no value or charm; it is for the seed-pods that we cherish it. Not that it needs much cherishing, and is even one of those amiable plants that will tolerate shade. Strugglers with shady gardens, or with difficult shaded areas, will doubtless note this point. The seed-pods are for late autumn and winter decoration indoors, for the seeds have the unusual property of not dropping out when the pod bursts open, and will last for a long time in a vase; they look fine, and warm, under a table-lamp on a bleak evening. Miss Gertrude Jekyll used to advise hanging the bunch upside down for a bit, to stiffen the stalks; I daresay she was right; she was usually right, and had an experimental mind.

Let me not claim for the gladdon iris that its crop of orange berries makes a subtle bunch or one which would appeal to flower-lovers of very delicate taste; it is frankly as coarse as it is showy, and has all the appearance of having been brought in by a pleased child after an afternoon's ramble through the copse. Nevertheless, its brightness is welcome, and its coarseness can be lightened by a few sprays of its companion, the berberis.

Iris foetidissima

NINE HUNDRED PEACHES

Some friends of mine planted a small peach tree six years ago. They stuck it in and left it to make what it could of itself. This year they have picked over 900 peaches from it, fine large fruits, excellent for dessert, for jam or for bottling. We usually associate peaches with a sunny wall – and how warm the rosy fruit looks, hanging against old brick of much the same colour – but this tree stands out in the open, unsheltered, unprotected, and unpruned. The branches had to be propped, they were so heavy; but apart from a generous mulch of manure, that was all the attention it got. A good reward, I thought, for so little trouble.

Of course, if you could find a sheltered corner, say in the angle formed by two hedges, giving protection from cold winds, it might do even better; and there is no doubt that if you threw a veil of tiffany or butter-muslin or even some old lace curtains over the blossom when frost threatens in April or May, you would be doing much to safeguard the crop. This would apply especially in a hard winter and a draughty spring. My friends treated their tree rough: they let it take its chance, and it took it. So I thought I would advise other people to try the same experiment.

After all, what do you risk? A guinea to buy the tree. Then you wait for a year or two, and then you start to pick the fruit. You get a couple of dozen after three years. After six years you get 900 – not a bad investment. It would certainly succeed in the Home Counties and in the South, and I have heard of a regular orchard of peaches in Essex, though I should not like to venture an opinion about the North. But, given a reasonably mild district, there seems no reason why this experiment should not be turned into profit as well as pleasure. The importation of foreign fruit has naturally not improved the English market, but the home grower can still sell peaches or nectarines and 900 sales would make a useful contribution to the current expenses involved in keeping up a garden.

THE BLUE DAISIES

People who have a frost-proof greenhouse in which to winter some tender plants, might well consider keeping a stock of the blue daisy, *Felicia amelloides*. It is a little shrub, or sub-shrub, about eighteen inches high, from South Africa, easily raised from seed or cuttings as a pot-plant, to set out in the open border towards the end of May, when it will flower continuously

Felicia amelloides

until the time comes to dig it up and repot it and carry it back into shelter for the winter. Its constant supply of starry, bright blue flowers makes it a very desirable asset in the summer border, even if it cannot claim to share the rich sapphire of the gentians. The forget-me-not comes closer within its range of colour; or some blue Northern eyes.

It is botanically related to the asters. *Aster amellus* is a familiar term in gardening language, but perhaps only a very small percentage of gardeners who talk glibly about *Aster amellus* realise that they are going right back to the poet Virgil, who in the first century B.C. gave the name *amellus* to a blue-flowered plant found wild on the banks of the River Mella in Italy. Thus do classical times connect with our present-day gardening. Rather romantically, I think, as well as classically.

There is another form of this pretty blue daisy which can be grown from seed as a half-hardy annual. This is *Felicia bergeriana*, the kingfisher daisy, well named since it really does suggest a flight of kingfishers stopped on the wing and held stationary for our enjoyment. No one could arrest a kingfisher in flight, that flash of blue; but the kingfisher daisy is the next best thing.

NOVEMBER

Forget not the bees in winter, though they sleep,
For winter's big with summer in her womb,
And when you plant your rose-trees, plant them deep,
Having regard to bushes all aflame,
And see the dusky promise of their bloom
In small red shoots, and let each redolent name —
Tuscany, Crested Cabbage, Cottage Maid —
Load with full June November's dank repose.

The Land

AUTUMN COLOURS

As we begin November, a note on autumn colour might not come amiss. From my window I gazed across the woods and watched oaks and beeches turning, but these are not trees that I myself have planted: they are just merely trees that have been there for two or three hundred years, sprung from a chance acorn or beech-mast. Sumptuous in their green-and-brown, a *verdure* tapestry on the grand scale of nature, they excelled my own puny efforts.

Still, my efforts were not too bad. I had a row of *Prunus sargentii* flaming above a rose-red vine, and some very ordinary azaleas which turn red, and some very ordinary thorns, *Crataegus crus-galli*, and *Cotinus coggygria* which turns into a little sunset all on its own. Then elsewhere I had *Parrotia persica*, a small tree which goes red and yellow, and *Euonymus alatus*, a Chinese form of our native spindle-tree, which grows no taller than six feet or so and turns bright pink, a really bright pink; and then the dwarf *Rosa nitida*, three to four feet high, creeping about on its own roots, making a small scarlet thicket in any corner where the evening light will catch it, never too much of an invader, never a nuisance, always a pleasure all the year round, but especially in autumn, with its red leaves, bristly red stems, and small red hips. I have loved *Rosa nitida* for many years, and have often wished to persuade other people to plant it more lavishly and lovingly. They would get their reward.

What other autumn colouring trees? We all know about liquidambar and *Nyssa sylvatica*, to be seen at their best and most mature in such old gardens as Sheffield Park in Sussex. We cannot aspire to such swagger planting within the short years of our tenancy. That is a thing of the past and of undiminished incomes. The most we

The entrance to Sissinghurst Castle looking towards the Tower

Thymus serpyllum

can do is to visit these great gardens and to reproduce very modestly what we see growing there and pick out for ourselves anything we regard as most showy for our own private gardens. I recall a vine, *Vitis coignetiae* it was, making a huge mound all over a dead tree, the size of a cottage almost, a thatch of big red shield-shaped leaves; and I thought: Now there's a thing anybody could grow. Why don't they? Over an unsightly shed, for instance.

Like all vines, it is extremely easy to propagate from any "eye", when the time comes to prune it in the winter. Stick a handful of prunings into a pot full of sand, and you will find that the majority of them will strike roots.

PLANNING A SMALL GARDEN

The problem of the small garden. I received a letter which went straight to my heart, more especially as it contained a plaintive cry that unintentionally scanned as a line of verse, "I never shall adapt my means to my desires". A perfectly good alexandrine, concisely expressing the feeling of millions, if not of millionaires.

The writer has a back garden fifty feet by thirty-five, and a front garden which he dismisses as being like any small villa in extent. How, he asks, would I harden my own heart if I had to decide between the demands of priority for the different seasons? Would I drop out one of the flowering periods altogether? No, I would not. I should always want at least one winter-flowering shrub, witch hazel for choice, and at least one tree of the cherry, *Prunus subhirtella* 'Autumnalis', giving branches to pick from November till March, and the yellow winter jasmine against a back wall of the house. Much use can be made of house walls for climbers, without robbing any space from the garden proper. I should have little narrow beds running round three sides of the house, south, east, and west, and these I should fill with bulbs of various kinds, dependent upon the taste of the owner, and dependent also upon the requirements of the bulbs, keeping the sun-loving kinds to the south and kinds more tolerant of shade, such as snowdrops and winter aconites, to the east and west.

I should cram my southerly bed with anemones, all opening to the sun, the blue Greek *Anemone blanda*, the Italian blue *apennina*, and with the exquisite *Anemone* 'St. Bavo', insufficiently grown yet so easy and self-sowing, of a beauty that far transcends the coarser blooms of *Anemone* 'St. Brigid' or even the handsome *Anemone* 'de Caen'. These narrow beds I should overplant with a variety of low-growing things, again dependent upon their choice of aspect, perhaps the creeping thymes to the south, making a red and lilac carpet of flower in late May and early June, perhaps the smaller violets to the east and west, but I should also leave spaces between them for the sowing of some chosen annuals, the blue cynoglossum and phacelia, also the 'Cambridge Blue' lobelia, and any other dwarf annuals as taste may dictate. These would make a summer display when the bulbs had died down, and would even persist into autumn if late sowings were made.

This leaves the centre of the plot free for any bed or side border in which to grow flowering shrubs or herbaceous perennials. The boundary hedges I should unquestionably make of some flowering subject. Some roses make an extremely effective hedge, the old striped 'Rosa Mundi', for instance, or 'Conditorum', more prettily known as 'Assemblage des Beautés'; and there are evergreen kinds of berberis, flowering in spring and fruiting in autumn. It should thus be feasible, in the smallest plot, to cover the whole year.

AMIABLE SAGES

The family of the sages is well known both in the kitchen garden and the flower garden. Some are aromatic herbs, scenting the hillsides in the sun of Mediterranean countries, and are associated in our minds with rough paths, goats, and olives. The sage is altogether an amiable plant; indeed, its Latin name, *Salvia*, comes from *salvere*, to save or heal, and one of its nicknames is *S. salvatrix*, which sounds very reassuring. The common clary, or *S. sclarea*, is also known as clear eye and see bright, not to be confused with eyebright, that tiny annual whose proper name is *Euphrasia*. The French bestow a very genial personality on clary by calling it simply Toute Bonne, which to me at any rate suggests a rosy old countrywoman in a blue apron.

The kitchen sages make decorative clumps, for they can be had with reddish or variegated leaves

Rosa gallica 'Versicolor'
('Rosa Mundi')

as well as the ordinary grey-green. The garden sages are useful for the herbaceous border. I do not mean that half-hardy bedding-out plant beloved of the makers of public gardens, *S. splendens*, which should be forbidden by law to all but the most skilful handlers. I mean such old favourites as *S. nemorosa*, a three-foot-high bushy grower whose blue-lipped flowers cluster amongst red-violet bracts and have the advantage of lasting a very long time in midsummer; or *S. grahamii*, equally familiar, with durable red flowers, a Mexican, reasonably but not absolutely hardy. A more recent introduction, not yet so well known as it should be, is *S. haematodes*, greatly to be recommended; it grows about five feet high in a cloud of pale blue rising very happily behind any grey-foliaged plant such as the old English lavender. This salvia grows readily from seed, especially if sown as soon as it ripens, and will in fact produce dozens of seedlings of its own accord. It is good for picking, if you bruise the stems or dip their tips for a few moments into boiling water.

Anybody with the time to spare should grow *S. patens*. It is a nuisance in the same way as a dahlia is a nuisance, because its tubers have to be lifted in autumn, stored in a frost-proof place, started into growth under glass in April, and planted out again at the end of May. The reason for this is not so much the tenderness of the tubers themselves as the risk that a late frost will destroy the young shoots; possibly the use of a cloche or hand-light might obviate this danger. The amazing azure of the flowers, however, compensates for any extra trouble. Like the gentians, they rival the luminosity of the blue bits in a stained-glass window.

REMEMBER THE NECTARINE

An inquiry from a correspondent reminds

Salvia haematodes

me of that delicious fruit, the nectarine, and as late autumn is the best time for planting it I thought some advice just now might not come amiss.

It is very odd that the nectarine should not be better known or more freely planted. We all know the peach, and the nectarine is nothing but a peach with a smooth skin instead of a downy skin. It was, in fact, reported by a Mr William Forsyth, writing in 1824, that he had "often heard of a peach and a nectarine growing on the same tree".

Shakespeare evidently did not know the nectarine, nor had he much to say about the peach. "Peach-coloured satin" is his only reference. Gervase Markham knew the nectarine, which he called nectaryas, noting in 1616 that it "delighted to be planted against a wall". Andrew Marvell knew it:

The nectarine and curious peach
Into my hands themselves do reach.

The origin of the peach and the nectarine is romantic enough to please anybody. *Prunus persica* is the botanical name, making it sound as though it grew wild in that most romantic of Asian countries. I have eaten it there, and have grown it from a stone saved from my breakfast in Shiraz; alas, it was sterile. As a matter of fact, it does not grow wild in Persia but in China, and probably arrived in Europe through Persia by one of the silk trade routes in the first century B.C.

One way or another, it did arrive in Europe, and was known to the Romans and even to our rude ancestors the Anglo-Saxons under the name *Perseoc-treou*. That takes its history a long way back.

Now it is all very well being romantic, but what people want is practical advice. If you intend to invest in either a peach or a nectarine, you must decide where you are going to plant it. If you have not got a lean-to glasshouse against a wall, the south wall of the dwelling-house is the best substitute, in full sun. This means that you must dig out a great hole to receive your plant and prepare the hole with a rich mixture of loam and sand and lime possibly in the form of rubble. It is always very important to prepare the site before the plant arrives: the site then has time to settle down.

Good drainage is essential. You will have to wire the wall for tying in the shoots, and remember that these trees need a great deal of water. The best varieties of the nectarine are 'Lord Napier', 'Humboldt', 'Early Rivers', 'Pineapple' and 'Elruge'.

CHRISTMAS LILY-OF-THE-VALLEY

A temptation and a suggestion reach me, hand in hand, in the shape of a leaflet about retarded crowns of lily-of-the-valley. If this leaflet did not come from one of the most reliable and reputable of our nurserymen I should mistrust it, for it sounds too good to be true. As it is, I accept their word that I can have lilies-of-the-valley in flower within three to four weeks of planting, at any time of the year, including just now when they would come in appropriately for Christmas.

All that you do is to order the plants, and plant them the moment they arrive, without any delay. They do not like to be left lying about, waiting. You can plant them either in a frame, provided that you can keep the night temperature up to the day, which is not easy unless you have bottom heat; or else in pots or in boxes not less than four inches in depth, which means that an ordinary seedbox won't do; or else in bowls filled with peat fibre, put into a warm cupboard of about 60°F, if you have such a thing.

I suppose that a hot-air linen cupboard would meet this requirement, and would keep them in the dark until five or six inches of growth had risen from the crowns. They must not be exposed to strong light until then, and in any case never to the rays of the sun. For the same reasons, of warmth and shade, I imagine that they could be successfully started in their boxes, pots, or bowls under the staging of a greenhouse. They must always be kept moist, and the tips of the crowns should not be covered with soil.

Incidentally, this is a good time to plant the outdoor lily-of-the-valley. A neighbour of mine, who has wide drifts of them among the azaleas and primulas of his beautiful woodland garden, says that he never plants them at all, but just throws them down on the surface with a very light covering of leaf-mould, and leaves them to find their own way down into the ground. I have not tried it, but the method certainly works well with him, probably because he has a soft rich spongy soil, intersected by little streams and offering small resistance to the roots as they feel their way about. They have queer habits; I tried to grow them under trees, which is their natural condition, but they seem to prefer coming up in the middle of a stony path. Plants are really most unpredictable.

The ordinary old English lily-of-the-valley has the sweetest scent of all, but the larger-flowered variety called 'Fortin's Giant' has its value, because it flowers rather later and thus prolongs the season by about a fortnight.

SCENTED BUDDLEIA

The common buddleia, *B. davidii*, is not so satisfactory a shrub as it ought to be. Indeed, its principal charm lies in its power of attracting butterflies, which has earned for it the name of butterfly bush, certainly an improvement on the official name it acquired in the seventeenth century from the Rev. Adam Buddle. True, there are some varieties far better than the type: *veitchiana*, and *magnifica*, and a more recent hybrid known as 'Royal Red', but on the whole they are plants of an ugly habit, leggy even if you cut them back in the spring, as you should. I greatly prefer *B. fallowiana*, or *B. nivea*, with their young growth white and woolly; or *B. alternifolia*, of very energetic but graceful growth, weeping almost to the ground in long wands, small leaf like a willow, and capable of being trained as a standard by the removal of all lower branches. It came to this country from China at the comparatively recent date of 1915, which perhaps explains why it is not more often seen as yet, although it can be increased very easily from cuttings, develops very rapidly, and has the advantage of flowering at an early age.

There is also *B. globosa*, flowering in masses of little yellow balls, quite different from the long tassels of the butterfly bush, and very useful as a climber to cover an unsightly shed or fence; and there is the beautiful *B. colvillei*, rosy-red, but, alas! not

Sorbus hupehensis

very dependable except in the warm counties.

It is, however, of the buddleia called *auriculata* that I want to write. Frankly it is not much to look at. You might call it greenish-white, but it would be more honest to call it a dirty white, almost grey. A South African, it is not entirely hardy grown as a bush in the open, but planted at the foot of a wall it will reach fifteen to twenty feet in a very few years, and in my garden survived the wicked winter of 1946-47. It should be given an inconspicuous place, out of sight until wanted, for it would be a pity to waste good wall space on so drab an object: I grow it in the kitchen garden on the east gable end of an old stable. The whole point of this buddleia which I describe with such apparent lack of enthusiasm is that it flowers in November when flowers are rare, and that it smells of honey. Its scent alone makes it worth while; hidden in a vase in a humble corner, it really makes you look round for a bowl of sweet alyssum as you enter the room.

BERRIES FOR BOWLS

At a time of year when we have to depend so much on berries, some of the sorbus group come in very useful. A particularly pleasing one, I think, is *Sorbus hupehensis*, found by E.H. Wilson in the mountainous Chinese province of Western Hupeh in 1910. Looking at photographs of that wild region, one marvels evermore at the devotion and endurance of those men to whom we owe so many of the plants we now take for granted. It is not to be wondered at that the local authorities often refused to believe that they wished to proceed in search of anything less valuable than gold.

Sorbus hupehensis, like most of the mountain ashes, bears its small round fruits in clusters, but unlike our native rowan the fruits are not red. They are ivory-white, but so strongly tinged with pink at the top as to give the impression of being wholly pink, an impression which is reinforced by the red stems. Each fruit, individually, looks like a tiny apple, no bigger than a currant, and if you cut it open you will find the seed corresponding to apple pips inside. These seeds should germinate freely, so anyone so minded could raise a plantation of his own. A seven-year-old tree should have attained about ten feet in height. The eventual height may go to thirty or forty feet, but probably none of us need worry about that.

This sorbus provides a change from the familiar rowan, and a tight bunch in a bowl on the table makes the prettiest decoration. Gazing into it, I thought it had a fairy-story quality. The tiny white-and-pink fruits might suddenly become detached and string themselves into rows of orient pearls. But I do not suppose that Ernest Henry Wilson had any such frivolous thoughts when he first discovered it growing on some rocky ledge in the mountains of Hupeh.

A note on *Amaryllis belladonna*. The amateur gardener who grows some bulbs of this November-flowering lily (yes, I know it is not a true lily, but as it usually goes by the name belladonna lily I have used the common description) has probably noticed that his bulbs occasionally take a year off and fail to produce any flowers at all, although they may have thrown up their leaves in the spring in the expected way. Unless he has by some means become aware of this idiosyncrasy, he may very understandably have assumed that something noxious had been happening to his bulbs underground during the summer, and may even have dug them up, only to find them as plump and healthy as ever. There is no cause for alarm. A friend of mine tells me that after she had lived nine years in her house, a magnificent clump of amaryllis suddenly appeared through a bush of pernettya which she herself had planted. Incidentally, the pink berries of the pernettya matched the rather harsh pink of the amaryllis as though placed there on purpose.

For those who, like myself, do not much care for the harsh pink, there is a white form they might find preferable.

NEW WAYS WITH CREEPERS

One does not, in the southern provinces of France, pick up many ideas adaptable to northern gardens; the climate is too different, not only because many desirable plants would not be hardy with us, but also because the strong sunshine beautifies groups of colour which at home would look only too like the bedding-out of a municipal garden. Scarlet salvia, cannas, and even begonias glow with an intensity that gives them a new character.

I did, however, note a way of using one very ordinary plant, and can see no reason why we should not follow a good example. This was our old friend the Virginia creeper. I have always thought it a potentially very handsome thing it itself, as sanguine in autumn as any maple, but not when we behold it glued against the wall of a red brick villa. Here in the South it is allowed to grow free, tumbling in cascades over some terrace or clambering through some dark green tree, to fall back in long loose strands of scarlet. Given its liberty it is as startling as the red tropaeolum which ramps in Scotland but is often recalcitrant in England. I can imagine it wreathing a holly, or hanging amongst the branches of *Quercus ilex* (holm oak) if you are so fortunate as to possess a fully grown one, or even scrambling along a rough hedge of thorn. Very often one finds such hedges with a holly left to grow high. I believe because country people retain an old superstition that it is unlucky to cut them down to hedge-level. However that may be, the sudden pyramid of scarlet and green would flare like a torch, especially when caught by the low rays of an autumnal sun.

I have laid emphasis on the advantage of some dark tree as a host for the creeper, because to my mind the combination of dark green and brilliant red is one of the most effective in nature, but I do recall once seeing a Virginia creeper that had found its way high into the branches of a silver birch. There it hung, pale pink and transparent in the delicacy of the white tree. It must have been a garden escape, for no one would have thought of planting it there, on the edge of a wood.

The same idea could be extended to some of the ornamental vines, for example *Vitis vinifera* 'Brandt'. Not enough use is made of ornamental vines in this country, nor have we learnt to grow them in the way they can best be used, as I could imagine them pouring loose and unrestricted, as I saw them treated, all careless and rampant over the terraces and parapets of ruined castle walls in south-western France.

STRAWBERRY TREES

The arbutus or strawberry tree is not very often seen in these islands, except in south-west Eire, where it grows wild, but it is an attractive evergreen of manageable size and accommodating disposition. True, most varieties object to lime, belonging as they do to the family of *Ericaceae*, like the heaths and the rhododendrons, but the one called *Arbutus unedo* can safely be planted in any reasonable soil.

To enumerate its virtues. It is, as I have said, evergreen. It will withstand sea gales, being tough and woody. It has an amusing, shaggy, reddish bark. It can be grown in the open as a shrub, or trained against a wall, which perhaps shows off the bark to its fullest advantage, especially if you can place it where the setting sun will strike on it, as on the trunk of a Scots pine. Its waxy, pinkish-white flowers, hanging like clusters of tiny bells among the dark green foliage, are useful for picking until the first frost of November browns them; a

Amaryllis belladonna

drawback which can be obviated by a hurried picking when frost threatens. And, to my mind, its greatest charm is that it bears flower and fruit at the same time, so that you get the strawberry-like berries dangling red beneath the pale flowers. These berries are edible, but I do not recommend them. According to Pliny, who confused it with the real strawberry, the word *unedo,* from *unum edo*, means "I eat one", thus indicating that you don't come back for more.

After its virtues, its only fault; it is not quite hardy enough for very cold districts, or for the North.

There is another arbutus called *menziesii*, which is the noble Madrona tree of California, reaching a height of 100 feet and more in its native home. I doubt if it would ever reach that height in England, though I must admit that the one I planted here in Kent some fifteen years ago is growing with alarming rapidity and has already obscured a ground-floor window; soon it will have attained the next floor, and

Arbutus unedo
and *Arbutus menziesii*

what do I do then? Let it grow as high as the roof, I suppose, and beyond. Its lovely bark, mahogany colour until it starts to peel, revealing an equally lovely olive-green underneath – gives me such pleasure that I could never bear to cut it down. Perhaps an exceptionally severe winter will deal with the problem, for it is marked with the dagger of warning, meaning "tender" in the catalogues.

There is also *Arbutus andrachne*, with the characteristic red bark, but this, again, is suitable only for favoured regions such as south and south-west England, parts of Wales, Northern Ireland, and south-west Eire. On the whole it is safer to stick to *Arbutus unedo*, so rewarding with its green leaves throughout the winter, and so pretty with its waxy racemes and scarlet fruits in autumn.

A NOVEMBER FLOURISH

Some weeks ago (to be precise, on October 2) I wrote that the blue trumpets of *Gentiana sino-ornata* had given great pleasure during September. I little knew, then, how I was under-estimating their value; so, in fairness to this lovely thing, I would like to state here and now, on this eighteenth day of November when I write this, that I have today picked at least two dozen blooms from my small patch. They had avoided the gales by cowering close to the ground, but they had suffered some degrees of frost; they looked miserable and shut up; I hesitated to pick them, thinking that they were finished for the year; they looked like rolled-up umbrellas; but now that I have brought them into a warm room and put them into a bowl under a lamp they have opened into the sapphire-blue one expects of the Mediterranean.

This mid-November bowl has so astonished me, and made me so happy, gazing at it, that I felt I must impart my delight to other people in the hope that they would begin to plant this gentian.

It is not easy to find flowers for this time of year. November and December are the worst months. One has to fall back upon the berried plants, and amongst these I think *Cotoneaster henryanus* is one of the best. It is a graceful grower, throwing out long, red-berried sprays, with dark green, pointed, leathery leaves of especial beauty. It is not fussy as to soil and will flourish either in sun or shade; in fact, it can even be trained against a north wall, which is always one of the most difficult sites to find plants for in any garden. *Berberis thunbergii*, either the dwarf form or the variety called 'Atropurpurea', both so well known that perhaps they need no recommendation, will also thrive in sun or shade, and at this time of year flame into the bonfire colours of autumn. They should be planted in clumps in some neglected corner, and be left to take care of themselves until the time comes to cut them for what professional florists call "indoor decoration", but what you and I call, more simply, something to fill the flower-vases with. They have the additional merit of lasting a very long time in water.

The leaves of the rugosa rose, 'Blanc Double de Coubert', also turn a very beautiful yellow at this time of year and are good for picking. This rose has every virtue: the flowers are intensely sweet-scented, they persist all through the summer, they are succeeded by bright red hips in autumn, as round as little apples, and the whole bush is a blaze of gold in November. The only disadvantage, for a small garden, might be the amount of room the bush takes up; it is a strong grower, like most of the rugosas, and will eventually spread to a width of four or five feet and to a height of a tall man. It is, however, very shapely, with its rounded head, and it never straggles.

*M*ORE FLOWERING HEDGES

To round off dark November, I will look ahead to future planting and write again about flowering hedges. Among them I would place pre-eminently the rose hedge, but that is perhaps a special theme demanding a list of suitable varieties. Some of the barberries make excellent hedges, flowering orange or yellow in spring and carrying a crop of dark berries in autumn, moreover they are thorny enough to repel most intruders, and they can be clipped as much or as little as you desire. *Berberis darwinii, B. stenophylla,* and *B. gagnepainii* are the three most frequently recommended, though if you want something less ordinary there is the blazing orange-red *B. linearifolia*. This species, however, is rather slow of growth.

The pyracantha or firethorns are less conspicuous for their flowers than for their berries, but in autumn when they are in full fruit they make a brilliant show. *P. rogersiana, P. angustifolia*, and *P.* 'Lalandei' are all suitable and cruelly armed. Among the cotoneasters, unarmed but berrying, are *C. franchetii*, which needs very little pruning, and *C. simonsii*, which can be cut harder if you want it shapely, though, of course, hard cutting means the loss of some of the fruit. Chaenomeles, commonly called japonica, can be grown as a hedge. I should like to see the variety *cathayensis* treated this way, for it is very spiny, and the enormous jade-green fruits always attract attention, and can be used for jam.

If you want a loose, informal hedge, intended purely for ornament and not for the exclusion of cattle and small boys, there are many of the flowering shrubs which will

Gentiana sino-ornata

serve the purpose. *Forsythia intermedia* draws a line of gold, and so does the single *Kerria japonica*, so much lighter and more peaceful than the double variety often seen in old gardens. Lilac and the sweet-scented *Philadelphus coronarius* can be grown as hedges instead of as single specimens; of a spreading habit, they take up a good deal of room and lilac is apt to sucker unless you make sure of getting it on its own roots. *Hypericum patulum*, a form of St John's Wort, especially the varieties called 'Forrestii' and 'Henryii', has a very long flowering season and does not mind a little shade. The deutzias will likewise tolerate some shade, and are charmingly pink and white in June, but they must not be pruned or you will lose next season's flowers. Fortunately they do not grow very tall or untidy.

DECEMBER

Then may you shoulder spade and hoe,
And heavy-booted homeward go,
For no new flowers shall be born
Save hellebore on Christmas morn,
And bare gold jasmine on the wall,
And violets, and soon the small
Blue netted iris, like a cry
Startling the sloth of February.

The Land

*J*UMPING TO IT INDOORS
   We are into December, Mid-winter-monath in old Saxon, and what a difficult time it is to produce flowers to fill even a few vases in the house. The winter-flowering cherry, *Prunus subhirtella* 'Autumnalis', is a great stand-by. I have been cutting small branches of it for two weeks past, standing them in water in a warm room, when the green buds surprisingly expand into the white, faintly-scented blossom suggestive of spring. This is a little tree which should be planted in every garden. It doesn't take up much space, and pays a rich dividend for picking from November until March. Even if frost catches some of the buds, it seems able, valiant little thing that it is, to create a fresh supply. This year, the winter cherry was in full flower in the open during the first fortnight of November; I picked bucketfuls of the long, white sprays; then came two nights of frost on November 15 and 16; the remaining blossom was very literally browned-off; I despaired of getting any more for weeks to come. But ten days later, when the weather had more or less recovered itself, a whole new batch of buds was ready to come out, and I got another bucketful as fresh and white and virgin as anything in May.

   There is a variety of this cherry called 'Autumnalis Rosea', slightly tinged with pink; I prefer the pure white myself, but that is a matter of taste.

   By the way, I suppose all those who like to have some flowers in their rooms even during the bleakest months are familiar with the hint of putting cut branches, such as this winter-flowering cherry, into almost boiling water? It makes them, in the common phrase, "jump to it".

   If you do not fancy the idea, you should consider an attractive woody little shrub,

The gate into the Rose Garden seen from the courtyard.

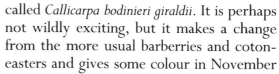

Prunus subhirtella 'Autumnalis'

called *Callicarpa bodinieri giraldii*. It is perhaps not wildly exciting, but it makes a change from the more usual barberries and cotoneasters and gives some colour in November and December. It, too, looks pretty in a glass under an electric lamp. The flowers, which come earlier in the year, are inconspicuous; the point is the deep-mauve berry, growing close to the stem in clusters, about the size of those tiny sugar-coated sweets which children call Hundreds and Thousands. I doubt if it would be hardy enough for very bleak or northern districts, though it should do well in a sunny corner in a line south of the Wash, as the weather reports say; it came undamaged through eighteen degrees of frost in my garden last winter.

There is one vital thing to remember about callicarpa: it is one of those sociable plants which like company of their own kind, so you must put at least two or three in a clump together, otherwise you won't get the berries. It is not a question of male and female plants, as it is with the Sea Buckthorn, which will not give its orange fruits unless married. The explanation appears to be simply that it enjoys a party.

This, of course, is true of many of the berrying shrubs, as well as of many human beings.

I am told that it makes a pretty pot-plant, grown on a single stem, when the berries cluster even more densely, all the way up. Here, again, it would be necessary to have several pots, not only one.

SEEDLINGS IN THE SLEEPING GARDEN

It is pleasant to see the garden laid to bed for the winter. Brown blankets of earth cover the secret roots. Nothing is seen overground, but a lot is going on underneath in preparation for the spring. It is a good plan, I think, to leave a heavy mulch of fallen leaves over the flowering shrubs instead of sweeping them all away. They serve the double purpose of providing protection against frost, and of eventually rotting down into the valuable humus that all plants need. There are leaves and leaves, of course, and not all of them will rot as quickly as others. Oak and beech are the best, to compost into leaf-mould in a large square pile; but any leaves will serve as a mulch over beds and borders throughout the hard months to come.

The professional gardener will raise objections. He will tell you that the leaves will "blow all over the place" as soon as a wind gets up. This is true up to a point, but can be prevented by a light scattering of soil or sand over the leaves to hold them down. This sort of objection may often be overcome by the application of some common sense. There are few people more obstinate than the professional or jobbing gardener. Stuck in his ideas, he won't budge.

It is also well worth while to search rather carefully for any stray seedlings which may have lain concealed beneath fallen leaves and the dead stalks of herbaceous stuff. It is surprising how many shrubs will thus reproduce themselves, even at some distance from their parent. They may be only a few inches high, when found, but by next spring they should start growing into useful little plants if you lift them with their roots intact and pot them up and sink the pots in a nursery row, either in ashes, sand, or ordinary soil. The point of sinking the pots is to safeguard them from being frozen hard, as they would be if left standing nakedly in the open.

Many of the commoner shrubs, such as the berberis, the cotoneasters, the brooms, the hypericums, and the buddleias, may often come to light in quantities and are just worth preserving if only to fill a gap in future or to give away.

I have also found more unexpected things than those: thriving little children of myrtle and the sweet-scented bay; the graceful indigofera; clerodendron of the turquoise-blue berries; *Solanum jasminoides*, that energetic climber; and even self-sown yews which if only I had had the sense and foresight to regiment along a drill years ago would by now have developed into a neat clippable hedge.

This is all satisfactory enough, but there are even more exciting possibilities. There is the chance that one of these stray seedlings may turn out to be better than its parent, or at any rate different. I believe I am right in saying that *Rosa highdownensis*, that lovely hybrid of *R. moyesii*, appeared accidentally in Sir Frederick Stern's garden at Highdown, and that *Caryopteris clandonensis* of a deeper blue than either *Caryopteris mongolica* or *C. incana*, was suddenly noticed by the present secretary of the R.H.S. in his own garden at Clandon. Of course, to spot these finds you have to be endowed with a certain degree of serendipity, meaning you have to be endowed with the faculty of "making discoveries by accident and sagacity" of something you were not deliberately in quest of.

This faculty involves knowledge, which is what Horace Walpole meant by serendipity when he coined his peculiar word. You have to know enough to recognise the novelty when you first see it, otherwise it might escape you altogether. You have to ensure also that the remorseless hoe does not scrape all your seedlings away into the heap destined for the barrow-load of rubbish. Scuffle about for yourself, before you let a jobbing gardener loose on beds or borders.

*T*HE BIRTH OF THE WHITE GARDEN
It is amusing to make one-colour gardens. They need not necessarily be

Callicarpa bodinieri giraldii

large, and they need not necessarily be enclosed, though the enclosure of a dark hedge is, of course, ideal. Failing this, any secluded corner will do, or even a strip of border running under a wall, perhaps the wall of the house. The site chosen must depend upon the general lay-out, the size of the garden, and the opportunities offered. And if you think that one colour would be monotonous, you can have a two- or even a three-colour garden provided the colours are happily married, which is sometimes easier of achievement in the vegetable than in the human world. You can have, for instance, the blues and the purples, or the yellows and the bronzes, with their attendant mauves and oranges, respectively. Personal taste alone will dictate what you choose.

For my own part, I am trying to make a grey-and-white garden. This is an experiment which I ardently hope may be successful, though I doubt it. One's best ideas seldom play up in practice to one's expectations, especially in gardening, where everything looks so well on paper and in the catalogues, but fails so lamentably in fulfilment after you have tucked your plants into the soil. Still, one hopes.

My grey-and-white garden will have the advantage of a high yew hedge behind it; a wall along one side, a strip of box edging along another side, and a path of old brick along the fourth side. It is, in fact, nothing more than a fairly large bed, which has now been divided into halves by a short path of grey flag-stones terminating in a rough wooden seat. When you sit on this seat, you will be turning your back to the yew hedge, and from there I hope you will survey a low sea of grey clumps of foliage, pierced here and there with tall white flowers. I visualise the white trumpets of dozens of Regale lilies, grown three years ago from seed, coming up through the grey of southernwood and artemisia and cotton-lavender, with grey-and-white edging plants such as *Dianthus* 'Mrs Sinkins' and the silvery mats of *Stachys lanata* or *olympica*, more familiar and so much nicer under its English names of Rabbit's Ears or Saviour's Flannel. There will be white pansies, and white paeonies, and white irises with their grey leaves . . . at least, I hope there will be all these things. I don't want to boast in advance about my grey-and-white garden. It may be a terrible failure. I wanted only to suggest that such experiments are worth trying, and that you can adapt them to your own taste and your own opportunities.

All the same, I cannot help hoping that the great ghostly barn-owl will sweep silently across a pale garden, next summer, in the twilight, the pale garden that I am now planting, under the first flakes of snow.

WINTER SPECTRES

Some years ago, I see that I mentioned *Rubus biflorus*. I described it as a white-washed bramble, and that was not far wrong, but there were two things I then omitted to say about this lovely phantom.

The first thing was that it carries a crop of pale yellow fruits like raspberries, which in fact they are, edible but very tasteless. The second thing was that it suckers most vigorously, running about on its own roots and coming up to ramp over a whole bed at the expense of other occupants. I had not foreseen this, so thought I had better add a word of warning.

If, however, you have a rough corner which can be given over, nothing could more rapidly or more ghostily fill it. How Walter de la Mare would have loved it. "These silver stems", he would have said, "should be visited by moonlight only", and he might have added that they reflected the snows of their Himalayan home. But as one is in the habit of visiting one's garden by daylight as well as by moonlight, I would suggest planting it if possible with a dark hedge as a background; ideally, in an angle formed by two dark hedges, and there let it have its way. Cut down the old fruiting canes as you would cut the kitchen-garden raspberry, and also cut down the more elderly canes to encourage the young shoots. They will need little encouragement, whether their progenitors get in the way or not.

Admittedly, this is not a plant for the small, neat garden unless kept under very severe control. It is too rampageous. It makes a thicket in no time, bleached, chalky, hoar as frost, whiter than bone. Which reminds me: if you grow *Abelia triflora*, that charming shrub hung with sweet-scented small trumpets of pinkish-white in June, have you noticed it in winter? It then takes on so different a character that you could scarcely believe it to be the plant you knew. Bare of leaf, it stands like an emaciated skeleton made out of ribs and phalanges and all the smaller and more brittle bones. You expect it to rattle in the wind.

Have I insisted too much upon these two spectres of the winter garden? I have written, perhaps, with an eye on those who see as much beauty in the steel-line engraving of winter as in the water-colours of spring or the oil-paintings of summer.

BIRDS, BUDS AND BERRIES

Have I ever mentioned, amongst early flowering shrubs, *Corylopsis pauciflora*? I don't think I have, so I will do so now. The corylopsis is a little shrub, not more than four or five feet high and about the same in width, gracefully hung with pale yellow flowers along the leafless twigs, March to April, a darling of prettiness. *Corylopsis*

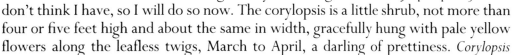

Rubus biflorus

spicata is much the same, but grows rather taller, up to six feet, and is, if anything, more frost-resistant. They are not particular as to soil, but they do like a sheltered position, if you can give it them, say with a backing of other wind-breaking shrubs against the prevailing wind.

Sparrows . . . They peck the buds off, so put a bit of old fruit-netting over the plants in October or November when the buds are forming. Sparrows are doing the same to my winter sweet this year, as never before: sheer mischief; an avian form of juvenile delinquency; so take the hint and protect the buds with netting before it is too late.

On the other hand, birds ignore the seldom-grown *Celastrus orbiculatus*. This is a rampant climber, which will writhe itself up into any old valueless fruit tree, apple or pear, or over the roof of a shed, or over any space not wanted for anything more choice. It is rather a dull green plant during the summer months; you would not notice it then at all; but in the autumn months of October and November it produces its butter-yellow berries which presently break open to show the orange seeds, garish as heraldry, *gules* and *or*, startling to pick for indoors when set in trails against dark wood panelling, but equally lovely against a white-painted wall.

It is a twisting thing. It wriggles itself into corkscrews, not to be disentangled, but this does

Celastrus orbiculatus

not matter because it never needs pruning unless you want to keep it under control. My only need has been to haul it down from a tree into which it was growing too vigorously; a young prunus, which would soon have been smothered. Planted at the foot of an old dead or dying tree, it can be left to find its way upwards and hang down in beaded swags, rich for indoor picking, like thousands of tiny Hunter's moons coming up over the eastern horizon on a frosty night.

*I*DEAS FOR ABUTILON

Christmas approaches, and perhaps I ought to be writing about mistletoe and holly, but I would rather go back to summer and try to revive some of its warm pleasures. We had the nastiest month of November, when the weather did everything it could think of: frost, snow, rain, floods, gales; but, even through that disagreeable span, one little climber persisted in flowering and I would like to record my gratitude. It had started flowering from early May onwards, and by December it was still in flower.

This was *Abutilon megapotamicum*. Its name is not so alarming. It derives from an Arabic word associated with the Mallows, a family to which our familiar garden hollyhocks belong; and *megapotamicum*, the great river, meaning the Amazon in Brazil.

Abutilon megapotamicum bears no resemblance at all to the hollyhocks as we know them in cottage gardens. It is a thing to train up against a sunny south wall, and if you should happen to have a whitewashed wall or even a wall of grey stone, it will show up to special advantage against it. It has long pointed leaves and a curiously shaped flower, dark red and yellow, somewhat like a fuchsia, hanging from flexible, limp, graceful sprays. It is on the tender side, not liking too many degrees of frost, so it should be covered over in winter. But perhaps you know all this already.

The idea I wanted to put forward is something that occurred to me accidentally, as gardening ideas do sometimes occur to one. I thought how pretty it might be to train an Abutilon as a standard. You see, it could be persuaded to weep downwards, like a weeping willow or a weeping cherry, if you grew it up on a short stem and constantly trimmed off all the side shoots it tried to make, till you got a big rounded head pouring downwards like a fountain dripping with the red and yellow flowers for months and months and months throughout the summer.

Is that a good idea? I have not tried it yet, but I intend to. Of course, for anyone who has the advantage of a greenhouse, however small and unheated, a little standard Abutilon in a big flower-pot might remain in flower well into the winter, and could be carried indoors for Christmas.

*T*HE CHRISTMAS ROSE

This seems a good occasion to mention the Christmas rose, *Helleborus niger*, in high Dutch called Christ's herb, "because it flowereth about the birth of our Lord". Its white flowers are, or should be, already on our tables. There is a variety called *altifolius*, which is considered superior, owing to its longer stalks; but it is often stained with a somewhat dirty pink, and I think the pure white is far lovelier.

Christmas roses like a rather moist, semi-shady place in rich soil, though they have no objection to lime; if you decide to plant some clumps you should do so as soon as they have finished flowering, which is another good reason for mentioning them now. If you already have old-established clumps, feed them well in February with a top-dressing of compost or rotted manure, or even a watering of liquid manure, and never let them get too dry in summer. Let me pass on a hint. If you happen to have an old clump in your garden, dig bits up and pot them into deep pots; put an inverted pot over each; keep them in the dark for a couple of weeks, and see what happens. You will find that the stalks are taller, and above all you will find that the flowers are of a purity and a whiteness they never achieved outside, not even under the protection of a cloche.

I know I shall be told that the Christmas rose does not like being disturbed. It is one of those plants with that reputation, but I am not at all sure that the reputation is wholly deserved. If you lift your clump with a large ball of soil, I guarantee that you will find it settling down again quite happily. It may not give of its best the first year, and for that reason it is advisable to stagger the potted clumps, some this year and some the next, planting them out into the open turn by turn.

The Christmas rose, although not a native of Britain, has been for centuries in our gardens. Spenser refers to it in the *Faerie Queene*, and it is described as early as 1597 in the *Herbal* of John Gerard, who considered that a purgation of hellebore was "good for mad and furious men". Such a decoction might still come in useful to-day. Perhaps Gerard was quoting Epictetus, who, writing in the early second century A.D., remarks that the more firmly deluded a madman is, the more hellebore he needs. Unfortunately, this serviceable plant is not very cheap to buy, but it is a very good investment because, to my positive knowledge, it will endure and even increase in strength for fifty years and more. It is also possible, and not difficult, to grow it from seed, but you should make sure of getting freshly ripened seed. Otherwise, you may despair of germination after twelve months have gone by and will crossly throw away a pan of perfectly viable seeds which only demanded a little more patience.

GOLDEN MISTLETOE

Why was it called golden, and why a bough, that grey-green tuffet, pearled and dotted with tiny moons? Apparently because it will turn golden if you keep it long enough, but as mistletoe usually comes down with the rest of the Christmas decorations it never gets the chance of assuming this different aspect of beauty.

Shakespeare called it baleful; but as everybody knows, it is possessed of most serviceable properties if only you treat it right. It can avert lightning and thunderbolts, witchcraft and sorcery; it can extinguish fire; it can discover gold buried in the earth; it can cure ulcers and epilepsy; it can stimulate fertility in women and cattle. On the other hand, if you do not treat it right, it can do dreadful things to you. It may even kill you, as it killed Balder the Beautiful, whose mother neglected to exact an oath from it "because it seemed too young to swear not to hurt her son".

The important thing, therefore, seems to be to learn as quickly and thoroughly as possible how to treat it right.

You must never cut it with iron, but always with gold. You must never let it touch the ground, but must catch it in a white cloth as it falls. This seems easy compared with the first stipulation, since even in these days most people do still possess a white cloth of some sort, a sheet, or a large handkerchief, whereas few of us can command a golden bagging-hook or even a knife with a blade of pure gold. You must never put it into a vase but must always suspend it, and after every traditional kiss the man must pick off one fruit (which is not a berry, although it looks like one) and when all the fruits have gone the magic of the kiss has gone also.

Folk tales? He would be a bold man who attempted to explain or to explain away such ancient and widespread superstitions, ranging from furthest Asia into Europe and Africa. Mysterious and magical throughout all countries and all centuries, these tales may be read in Sir James Frazer's monumental work in which he honoured that queer parasite, the mistletoe, with the title 'The Golden Bough'.

So here, in this short essay, let me concentrate rather on some botanical facts which Sir James Frazer disregards, and try to correct some popular misconceptions about the nature of the mistletoe.

We think of it as a parasite, but it is not a true parasite, only a semi-parasite, meaning that it does not entirely depend upon its host for nourishment, but gains some of its life from its own leaves. It belongs to an exceptional family, the *Lorantha-ceae*, comprising more than five hundred members, only one of which is a British-born subject: *Viscum album*: the Latin name for our English mistletoe.

The mistletoe, as we know it, grows on some trees and not on others. The worst mistake that we make is to believe that it grows most freely on the oak. It seldom does; and that is the reason why the Druids particularly esteemed the oak-borne mistletoe, for this was a rarity and thus had a special value. The mistletoe prefers the soft-barked trees: the apple, the ash, the hawthorn, the birch, the poplar, the willow, the

Helleborus niger

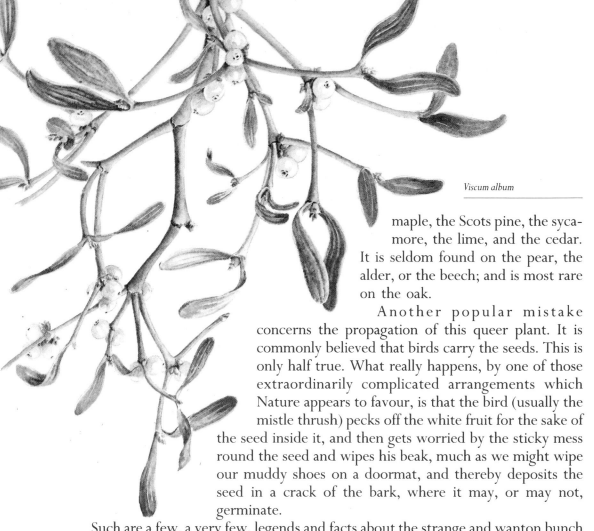

Viscum album

maple, the Scots pine, the syca-
more, the lime, and the cedar.
It is seldom found on the pear, the
alder, or the beech; and is most rare
on the oak.

Another popular mistake
concerns the propagation of this queer plant. It is
commonly believed that birds carry the seeds. This is
only half true. What really happens, by one of those
extraordinarily complicated arrangements which
Nature appears to favour, is that the bird (usually the
mistle thrush) pecks off the white fruit for the sake of
the seed inside it, and then gets worried by the sticky mess
round the seed and wipes his beak, much as we might wipe
our muddy shoes on a doormat, and thereby deposits the
seed in a crack of the bark, where it may, or may not,
germinate.

Such are a few, a very few, legends and facts about the strange and wanton bunch
we shall hang somewhere in our house at Christmas.

THE NOT-SO-SMALL SYRINGA

How comforting it is to feel that we still have at least three months before us in
which to plant the shrubs we had forgotten. These after-thoughts can safely go in at
any time up to next March, in fact most evergreens prefer to wait until the soil is
likely to start warming up. This reflection gives us a sense of respite and reprieve.

One of the most charming small shrubs for the rock garden is *Syringa palibiniana*. I
do resent having to call a thing syringa when what I really mean is lilac, but I cannot
go against the dictum of my betters. *Syringa palibiniana*, from Korea, resembles what
we should consider a miniature lilac, and the great point about it is its remarkable
fragrance. Bury your face in its neat rounded top in May if you want to get all the
distilled scent of every dew-drenched lilac you ever sniffed. It comes high in the list
of my garden darlings.

Perhaps I ought to qualify the term small or miniature shrub, since this is likely to
lead to confusion. Most nurserymen who list it claim that it grows only to three foot
high. This is wrong, since in fact it will eventually grow to about eight foot, a very
different matter. I think what has happened in the case of this syringa is that it starts
to flower so profusely and at so young an age that a dwarf habit has been too rashly

assumed.

What, then, are we to do? Obviously, we can't burden a small rock-garden with a shrub that intends to grow far taller than its companions or even than ourselves. There seems to be only one answer: plant it, enjoy it, and when it gets above itself, dig it up and replant it in some open place where it can grow away to its Korean heart's content.

I might add that some people claim that you can keep it clipped to the size you want. I have, for the time being, put it amongst some daphnes of a similar round-headed type, *Daphne retusa* and *collina*, and have inter-planted them with a handful of the pink-and-white striped *Tulipa clusiana*, the lady tulip. They should look pretty together, if only my scheme comes off. Alas, how seldom do these little schemes come off. Something will go wrong; some puppy will bury a bone; some mouse will eat the bulbs; some mole will heave the daphnes and the lilac out of the ground.

Still, no gardener would be a gardener if he did not live in hope.

PLANT SUPPLIERS

Alpines and Small Herbaceous Plants

W. E. Ingwersen
Grevetye Nurseries
East Grinstead
Sussex

E. Parker-Jervis
Marten's Hall Farm
Longworth
Abingdon
Oxfordshire

Stonecrop
Cold Spring
N.Y. 10516

Border Plants

Beth Chatto
White Barn House
Elmstead Market
Colchester
Essex

Blackthorne Gardens
48 Quincy Street
Holbrook
Mass. 02343

Bressingham Nurseries
Diss
Norfolk

Careby Manor Gardens
Careby
Stamford
Lincolnshire

T. Carlile Ltd
Carlile's Corner
Twyford
Reading
Berkshire

Sandwich Nurseries
Dover Road
Sandwich
Kent

St Bridget Nurseries Ltd
Old Rydon Lane
Exeter
Devon EX2 7JY

Bulbs

J. Amand
19 Beethoven Street
London W.10

Breck's
6523 North Glena Road
Peoria
Illinois 61632

Van Bourgondian Bros.
P.O. Box A
245 Farmingdale Road
Route 109, Babylon
Long Island
N.Y. 11702

Van Tubergen
304A Upper Richmond Road
    West,
London S.W.14

Wallace and Barr
Marden
Kent

Clematis

Blackthorne Gardens
48 Quincy Street
Holbrook
Mass. 02343

Fisks
Saxmundham
Suffolk

Treasures of Tenbury
Tenbury Wells
Worcestershire

Herbs

Hollington Nurseries Ltd
Woolton Hill
Newbury
Berkshire

Roses, including Old Fashioned varieties

Anderson's Rose Nurseries
Friarsfield Road
Cults
Aberdeen

Armstrong's Roses
15 Knockboy Road
Broughshane
Co. Antrim
N. Ireland

David Austin Roses
Bowling Green Lane
Albrighton
Wolverhampton WV7 3HB

Peter Beales Roses
London Road
Attleborough
Norfolk

R. Harkness & Co Ltd
The Rose Gardens
Hitchin
Hertfordshire

Hyrons Nursery & Garden
    Centre
Woodside Road
Amersham
Buckinghamshire

Rearsby Roses
Melton Road
Rearsby
Leics LE7 8YP

Roses of Yesterday and Today
802 Brown's Valley Road
Watsonville
California 95076

St Bridget Nurseries Ltd
Old Rydon Lane
Exeter
Devon EX2 7JY

Seeds

Alpina Research
18544 26th NE
Seattle
WA 98155

Thomas Butcher
60 Wickham Road
Shirley
Croydon
Surrey

Samuel Dobie
Upper Dee Mills
Llangollen
Clwyd
Wales

Thompson and Morgan
London Road
Ipswich
Suffolk

Thompson and Morgan
P.O. Box 100 Farmingdale
New Jersey 07727

W. S. Unwin
Histon
Cambridge

Trees and Shrubs

Burncoose and Southdown
   Nurseries
Gwennap
Redruth
Cornwall

Hilliers
Ampfield House
Romsey
Hampshire

Notcutts
Woodbridge
Suffolk

R. V. Roger Ltd
The Nurseries
Whitby Road
Pickering
North Yorkshire

Sherrards
Wantage Road
Donnington
Newbury
Berkshire

St Bridget Nurseries Ltd
Old Rydon Lane
Exeter
Devon EX2 7JY

Wayside Gardens
Hodges
South Carolina 29695

Weston Nurseries
East Main Street
Route 135
Hopkinton
Mass. 01748

INDEX

ACKNOWLEDGEMENTS

The Publishers would like to thank Nigel Nicolson, Pamela Schwerdt and The National Trust both for permission to take photographs at Sissinghurst Castle and for their enormous help in the preparation of this book.

The Publishers would like to thank the following organisations and individuals for their help in providing reference, plant specimens and advice for the illustration of the book: M.J. & R.D. Allen Nurseries, Hornchurch; Blooms of Bressingham Gardens, Norfolk; Borough of Brighton Parks and Gardens Dept; The British Iris Society; Broadleigh Gardens, Somerset; Marion Buist; Capel Manor Horticultural and Environmental Centre, Herts; Careby Manor Gardens, Lincolnshire; John Costen; Enterprise House Gardens; Four Seasons Nursery, Norwich; Mrs Hewitt; Hillier Nurseries (Winchester) Ltd; King's Florist, Walthamstow; Lee Valley Regional Park Authority; The Lindley Library, Royal Horticultural Society; Mrs Lowe; Edith Lynes; Edna Morris; National Council for the Conservation of Plants and Gardens; The National Trust; Ramparts Nursery, Colchester; Rearsby Roses; The Royal Botanic Gardens, Edinburgh; The Royal Botanic Gardens, Kew; The Royal Botanic Gardens, Wakehurst Place, Haywards Heath; The Royal Horticultural Society's Garden, Wisley; The Royal National Rose Society; Mrs Jean Sambrook; Rosemary Stille; Ron Treadgold; Muriel Walker; Emma Wilson; Rosemary Woods.